THE BACK SIDE
OF SATAN

THE BACK SIDE OF SATAN

by
Morris Cerullo

CREATION HOUSE
CAROL STREAM, ILLINOIS

FIRST EDITION

Library of Congress Catalog Number: 72-94922

ACKNOWLEDGMENT: All Biblical quotations taken from *New American Standard Bible* by permission of Lockman Foundation, La Habra, California.

v

Commendation

I want to express my deepest appreciation to Jean Jolly who spent many long hours laboring over this manuscript to bring it to its completed form. Though a member of my staff, she went far beyond the call of duty in her devotion to this project.

Morris Cerullo

Contents

PREFACE

Pinpointing the Enemy

As I stepped off a plane in India several years ago, I was met by my oldest son, who had traveled there with my advance team.

His face was white. He looked terrible—I thought I was seeing a ghost.

"David, what's wrong?" I asked.

"Dad, I don't know!" he said. "There's something in the air here. There is just something about this place that is making me sick. I don't understand it."

I understood it.

I had been to India before. I knew of the countless false gods that are worshiped by the Indian people. The oppression of these demon spirits is so thick you can feel it in the air. I knew this was what was making David sick.

As I travailed in prayer in my room for the mass evangelistic crusade I was to conduct there, something came over me that I had never felt before. I felt as though I were being literally torn apart in my inner being. I cannot describe the scene. Alone with God, I began to call out certain things by name and bind them in the name of Jesus: the spirits of sin, the spirits of sickness, the spirits of religion, the spirits of the false cults, the spirit of idol worship.

This went on for hours. Finally, victory came. We went through our whole campaign in India without one problem.

What God revealed to me during this time is one of the reasons behind this book.

I had been on the foreign field for twelve years prior to this experience. I was already well aware of what the church calls "demon powers." When I went into these countries, the anguish I went through in prayer in order to win a victory was indescribable. I struggled in such prayer because I knew I was combating special forces. I knew I was coming to grips with the supernatural powers of the enemy! I knew that these powers must be defeated in prayer before I ever left the prayer room!

However, I had never applied this principle in America; because here, you see, we think of ourselves as civilized people. We are educated people. So I used an entirely different approach at home than I did on the foreign field.

Now, however, I felt God speaking to my heart that this key, the key used for such victories on the foreign field, was also the key for victories in America.

The Lord said to me, "Son, you must realize that in the United States of America you're not dealing just with ideologies. You're not dealing with rebellious youth who are disenchanted with the hypocrisy of their parents. You're not dealing with kids who are trying to tear down the establishment. You're not just dealing with the drug culture.

"If you will go deep to the root of the problem, you will find that you're in a *spiritual* battle."

Spirits!

Small wonder that Paul, under the inspiration of the Holy Spirit, penned this strong warning in the sixth chapter of Ephesians: "For our struggle is not against flesh and blood, but against the rulers, against the powers, against the world forces of this darkness, against the spiritual forces of wickedness in the heavenly places." (v. 12)

I began to realize that there were tremendous spirit forces working in America to tear down the structure of our society. In fact, I believe with all my heart that the devil has assigned special spirits to this task.

One of the devious ways in which these spirits are working is to draw young people, as well as older folk, by use of the supernatural, into snares of occultism and Satan worship. This is a spirit that is coming more and more upon America. We see it everywhere.

Someone said to me, "Reverend Cerullo, we don't mention the word 'spirits' in our church anymore because my pastor says we are not to scare people."

Let me ask you this: *How can you fight an enemy you have not marked? How can you fight an enemy when you close your eyes and pretend he does not exist?*

He is here! The fight is on! And more and more of our American young people are becoming involved as this spirit sweeps through America.

At our Youth Action Center in San Diego, which is our youth outreach program with a twenty-four-hour hotline counseling service, we have seen a marked increase in calls from those who have become involved in occult practices and are in desperate need of help. At this writing there are several young people manning the telephones at the center who have been delivered from these satanic practices.

One young woman, who became one of our dedicated helpers, was involved in Satan worship for ten years. She has been delivered by the power of God. Now she, and others like her, are seeking to help those who have been similarly entangled.

It is my prayerful hope that this book, assembled after long research, will serve both as a warning to those tempted to taste the dark powers of Satan's underworld, and as a help to those who have already been enslaved and would like to be free.

To the ensnared I say, "You shall know the truth, and the truth shall make you free." (John 8:32) Jesus Christ is the Truth. He is the Answer. The Holy Spirit is the Power that enables us to break every fetter of the devil.

There are many faces of Satan. . . .

The Bible says he disguises himself as "an angel of light." (2 Corinthians 11:14) He is also called "a deceiver" in Revelation 20:8 and Revelation 12:9, in which it is said of him that he "deceives the whole world."

Most of man's problems, dilemmas, and even his sicknesses and sorrows can be traced to the invasion of spirits into men's lives. These spirits, whether they are negative thoughts, hatreds, prejudices, lusts, or inordinate passions, are real. They are tearing at the life style and stream of American Puritan heritage.

Thank God, we have a greater power than the devil. In 1 John 4:4 the Bible says, "You are from God, little children, and have overcome them; because greater is He who is in you than he who is in the world."

Through pinpointing our enemy and taking dominion over him in the authority of Christ, we can put the enemy on the run. That's why I selected the title *The Back Side of Satan* for this book.

May God bless this book to your heart is my earnest prayer.

Morris Cerullo
San Diego, California

1

Personal Encounter

The air of the stadium in Haiti was electric as time drew near for the opening service of the crusade which we had been invited by President Francois Duvalier to conduct in that country.

Five thousand people were jammed against the platform we had erected. Another ten thousand were packed into the stands.

Scattered through the crowd were 300 Haitian voodoo witch doctors whose plan was to create havoc, wreck the platform, and kill whomever they could—mainly me!

As the Christian leaders with whom I was making the trip sought to open the meeting and give testimonies, these red-shirted voodoo doctors began their rhythmic chant, "Boom . . . boom . . . boom . . . boom. Boom . . . boom . . . boom . . . boom." It was havoc. I could tell that Satan had really unleashed a host of spirits against this work of God.

A few hours earlier, when we had arrived in Haiti, a long string of limousines was waiting to take us on a parade through the city to our hotel. I was in a car with high officials including Senator Arthur Bonhomme and a general.

This was in 1960. I didn't know anything about Haiti

then. At that time I had only a few years of overseas experience in conducting foreign crusades. I'd been in the Philippines and in the Orient, and had had some large and successful meetings there.

Here in Haiti something different was happening. I felt a sickness in the pit of my stomach. I turned to the others and said, "Pull this car out of the motorcade."

"What do you mean?" The official was surprised. "We're going to take you by the palace!"

"*I can't tell you why*—but get me to my hotel." I knew the Lord was speaking to me.

They dropped me off at my hotel and took care of my reservations. I went to my room without stopping to unpack my bags, I got on my knees and began to pray.

"God," I prayed, "something's wrong here. This is not a sickness. This is a spiritual thing. You're wanting to speak to me."

That's true. The Lord spoke to me, not in an audible voice, but in my spirit.

"God," I said aloud, "what's wrong?"

The answer came readily back. *Tonight there are going to be 300 witch doctors at the crusade. You'll know them because they will wear red shirts. They're going to scatter themselves throughout this congregation, and they're there for the purpose of killing you.*

We had landed in Haiti in the middle of the Mardi Gras season. At this occasion there were seven Sunday nights in a row when wild celebrating went on. Almost a hundered thousand people were out on the streets in Port-au-Prince for those Sunday nights, reveling, drinking, engaging in all sorts of sexual expression and voodoo rites. Women were raped openly, with no interference, in one evening perhaps two to five thousand women.

We arrived in Haiti on the third Sunday of the Mardi Gras season. The witch doctors had already seen our publicity and announcements of the meetings, and they were mad.

They're going to come out to kill you, God said to me.

"Lord," I said, "thank you for telling me. I don't mind being a martyr if you want me to die." I had already faced just about everything there was to face. The stories of dangers I could tell would make your hair stand on end.

So I prayed, "Lord, if you want me to, I'll die." I meant it.

Then God said — (I'll quote this exactly without changing one word): *Son, I want you to remember something when you are there tonight. The words you speak will be exactly as if I had spoken it, and I will bring it to pass.*

In the evening I went out on the platform before thousands of jammed-in people. The witch doctors had everything torn up and the scene was chaos.

On the platform were seated dignitaries and their wives, including generals, senators, and other officials. I got up to speak.

Every time I'd start to talk, the witch doctors would start that chant again, "Boom . . . boom . . . boom . . . boom." And it went on. "Boom . . . boom . . . boom . . . boom." The emotions of the people were being stirred higher and higher. At this rate they were being worked into such a frenzy that soon they would probably rush up against the platform—tear it down and try to kill me.

I turned around for my interpreter who was a Bible school boy named "Nelson." Pointing my finger at him I said, "Son, I want you to interpret what I say—every word. Don't you dare change a single word. Not one syllable!"

"Yes, sir! Yes, sir! Yes, sir!" he agreed.

I called for the attention of the people, and I began. "God, the true God, has sent me to Haiti," I declared boldly. "The devil, who is against God, wants to keep you in bondage, for he has sent hundreds of witch doctors here tonight to kill me and to destroy this meeting.

"Now, so you will know how I know—the living God told me!"

The place was getting quiet now.

I continued. "We're going to find out right here tonight who has the greater power, the living God whom I serve, or the devil, who sent these witch doctors."

They were all attention now.

"The God that I came here to tell you about is a loving

3

God, and He sent me here to tell you that He loves you so much that He wants to take away your sins, take away your burdens, and take away your sicknesses. I've come here to tell you how you can be free of all those things."

Then I added, "But that same God is a God of judgment. The next witch doctor, or any person who opens his mouth to destroy this meeting in any way, shape, or form, before all these officials"—and I indicated all the dignitaries sitting on the platform—I will not be responsible for when they carry you out of this stadium *dead*."

You could have heard a pin drop. It remained silent for the whole meeting.

I preached only about fifteen or twenty minutes. The power of God came upon all those heathen voodoo people.

All of a sudden something happened at the fringe of the crowd; about 5,000 people jammed onto the field. Someone began to scream and started pushing a baby up into the air.

The people were so packed together that if one of them moved, all of them moved; that's no exaggeration. The whole crowd was swaying back and forth, side by side, and began passing the baby along, overhead, toward the platform.

Someone began to scream, "Brother Cerullo, this baby was born blind, and now it's seeing! It's seeing!"

The baby finally reached the platform, and we began to test out the healing. Somehow the baby's mother and father managed to slip through the crowd to the front. It was true. This baby—which had been born blind—was now seeing.

A government official stood up. I can see him to this day, dressed in the uniform of a soldier. I don't remember what his rank was, but it must have been high because he was seated on the platform.

I can see him even now, standing there with his hands up to his head, looking in astonishment at that baby and literally shaking with emotion.

"Mr. Cerullo," he whispered hoarsely, "Mr. Cerullo, that's my neighbor!"

Then the meeting broke wide open. The leading witch doctors were converted. Our crusade really started ministering after that miracle. We stayed there for three weeks,

4

and God shook that whole nation. It has never been the same since.

Now this is the kind of God we serve. His power is greater than the power of voodooism, greater than the power of Hinduism or any other spirit power of Satan. Through God, we can come against all these other evil powers and spirits and see the victory every time.

I've seen it happen over and over.

In Asunción, Paraguay, village leaders came into our meetings with rocks in their hands. They brought four or five hundred kids with them into the meeting, all armed with rocks.

When I got there, the grounds were full of people, but the platform was empty. All the missionaries and other officials had gone underneath the platform because people had been throwing eggs at them.

"Brother Cerullo," my helpers warned me, "hundreds of kids are here with rocks. They're going to stone you!"

I walked right out onto that platform and stood up before the crowd, ignoring the people who wanted to harm me. I opened my Bible and began to speak.

As I spoke, there came the sounds of rocks hitting the ground. People just opened their hands and dropped their stones. There was not one disturbance to hurt me or stop the message.

As in this case, God has proved Himself over and over in confrontations with evil forces. Not only have I seen God triumph for whole meetings such as I have related, but in individual lives.

In our first Miami crusade, we had a lady delivered instantaneously from the grip of voodooism. In Oakland, just recently, a mother and two daughters came across the platform, and all three were set free from evil spirits which had plagued them.

I remember especially a boy I met several years ago in Guayaquil, Ecuador. Maybe I remember him so vividly because, like me, he was an orphan.

Alfredo Nunoz and his wife operated a small restaurant on the waterfront of Guayaquil. One day they spotted a young boy wandering aimlessly around during an equatorial downpour. They called him to come in out of the rain.

But what a tragedy! They found that the boy could not speak. He seemed to hear, but an expression of terrible frustration covered his face when he attempted to speak. He couldn't utter even one sound.

They gave the boy food and dry clothing and let him sleep in a small loft over the restaurant for a few nights. Alfredo and his wife also gave him love and understanding, and before long they took the boy into their own home to live with them and their three children.

Three months later, they saw an ad in the local newspapers advertising our meetings and telling how this American preacher believed in praying for the sick and afflicted as it was done in the Bible. Alfredo and his wife felt that they must get the boy to that meeting.

After preaching a message of salvation and faith in God that night, I took authority in the name of Jesus and commanded deaf and dumb demons to come out.

In the middle of the prayer, the boy felt something he had never experienced before! A warm Presence began to come upon his shoulders as though two hands were pressed upon him from behind. As this Presence became more intense, the boy felt something being lifted. He felt lighter! A terrible "presence" that had been his companion for eight long years was lifting, giving place to this new warmth that he felt.

At that moment of complete separation, all fear left the boy, and a great moment of release took place. His tongue was loosed! He could make sounds! He could speak! The neighbor who had brought him was so amazed he could hardly speak himself.

Afterwards, the boy's story began to unfold. Very early in his childhood he had been abandoned by his mother, and he could not recall seeing her face. When he was seven, Marcello lived with his father in Quito, the capital of Ecuador.

One evening he was home alone when a harsh knock came at the door and he was commanded to open it up. Two strange men rushed into the dimly lit room and roughly pushed the boy aside, terrifying him by their actions. His impressionable young mind was so severely shaken by this traumatic experience that it was several days before he was able to return to the world of reality. Then he found that his vocal chords were so bound by fear that he could not speak.

After this, Marcello's father no longer wanted him around. Alfredo was put out into the cold streets. Later the boy obtained a ride to Guayaquil, which had a warmer climate. For eight years he had lived in the streets there and eaten from garbage cans.

After that first service, God continued to work in that young man, and by the time of the closing service in that city, he stood before the vast audience of more than 30,000 persons and told how Christ had healed him. He also told how he planned to preach the gospel of the resurrection power of Jesus Christ.

That is just one example of literally thousands of deliverances we have seen in this ministry from the bondage of Satan.

All my life, since I accepted Christ at the age of fourteen while I was in an orthodox Jewish orphanage in New Jersey, I have lived in a spiritual world.

I know God is a spirit and that He wants us to worship Him in our spirits. We can read that in the Bible in John 4:24 where Jesus says, "God is spirit; and those who worship Him must worship in spirit and truth."

I have known also that Satan has his evil spirits which he controls and uses to bind and destroy people.

For over twenty-five years, since I was fifteen years old, I have preached that God is real, and that the devil is real. And I have preached that God's power is greater than the devil's. I have told men and women that they don't have to be bound by Satan.

Literally thousands of people have come across our platform in crusades around the world and have been instantaneously set free from some affliction or need they had in their lives by the power of God.

If there is one keynote to our ministry, it is *authority*, for that is what God has given us in the name of Jesus.

It is not the authority of man. Over and over, audiences around the world have heard me say, "This is not the work of a man. This is not the work of Morris Cerullo. This is the work of the Holy Spirit."

7

We give God the honor and praise for everything that is done. If God will do it for one, He will do it for others, whether on the fields of Argentina or India or Ecuador, or in the cities of Phoenix or Miami or Denver.

No matter where the scene is set or what the circumstances are, in the showdown, God's power is greater than all the power of the enemy!

2

The New Face of Satan

In eons past, before the advent of man, one of the angels of God made a boast. He said, "I will raise my throne above the stars of God . . . I will make myself like the Most High." (Isaiah 14:13-14)

This angel was Lucifer, the star of the morning, who was cast out of heaven by God. We know him today as Satan, or the devil.

Satan's ambition was clear from the very beginning. He wanted to be worshiped.

Put out of heaven because of his pride and rebellion, the devil has continued to nourish this ambition. He still wants to be worshiped. It's his plan to get every man to rebel against God, if possible, and to turn towards Satan.

Many times, Satan skillfully disguises his plans and purposes, for remember we are warned that he is transformed into an "angel of light." (2 Corinthians 11:14)

He uses many faces today, many disguises. But underneath it all, he is still the "adversary," the "roaring lion seeking someone to devour." (1 Peter 5:8)

He is not always as blatantly open as when he confronted Jesus and tried to get Jesus to fall down and worship him. He can come in a variety of ways, including the most innocent looking ones in the world! In the story of the fall of man as recorded in the book of Genesis, Satan used the form of a serpent, the "most subtle" of all the creatures.

If Satan can't win the whole battle in one sweep, he is content to win it an inch at a time. But he will keep on until he has won the whole prize if possible.

If he cannot get people to fall down and worship him openly at his first appearance, he will try to seduce them with some little "harmless pleasure" containing a well-hidden hook!

This is what is happening in America today on the occult scene.

Some have fallen already to the lowest degradation of worshiping Satan openly, engaging in the most vile obscenities and blasphemies imaginable. Many of these cannot be told in this book! I wouldn't speak of them, or write them.

But many—millions even—are nibbling at the tempting morsels of supernatural enjoyment held out to them by Satan, and are gradually becoming ensnared in the occult to the point of physical and mental anguish, mental derangement, and the committing of violent crimes.

The recent records of violent crimes are full of those committed by people who have been involved in the occult scene. Look at these startling examples.

A thirty-one-year-old California schoolteacher, mother of five children, was abducted by five drug addicts. She was stabbed twenty times. Her body was dismembered by a young man who later admitted that he worshiped Satan.

In Montana, a twenty-two-year-old social service worker picked up a hitchhiker near Yellowstone National Park. The rider shot his victim in the back of the head, cut off his head, arms and legs, and then allegedly ate some of the still warm heart. He told police that he worshiped Satan.

In Florida, a sixty-nine-year-old pensioner in Miami Beach was stabbed to death by a young woman who later told reporters she had been worshiping Satan for the past five years.

In New Jersey, a twenty-year-old factory worker induced two teenager friends to assist him in killing himself so that he could "come back in another life to lead forty legions of demons."

In California, the brutal murders of actress Sharon Tate and her friends made ugly headlines which shocked the nation. It was later revealed that both the infamous killer Charles Manson and some of the victims in the case had long histories of occult involvement.

Shocking as these cases may be, they are but a few of the many instances where witchcraft, Satanism, and other types of occult practices are involved in a growing number of violent crimes, spreading ominous shadows across the face of America and around the world.

You may think these are extreme cases, but they had their start somewhere. Perhaps they even started in a so-called "search for truth," or in someone's search "for kicks."

But the hook was there. Somehow the victim was ensnared, and eventually, the mask was ripped off. Behind it all was man's age-old enemy, Satan, still seeking to kill and to destroy and to devour.

The Old Testament and ancient history contain many references to witchcraft, sorcery, astrology, and other forms of the occult. The Bible, of course, lays down strict "do nots" for those who would get involved in these things. God commanded the children of Israel to have nothing to do with this type of activity.

> There shall not be found among you anyone who makes his son or his daughter pass through the fire, one who uses divination, one who practices witchcraft, or one who interprets omens, or a sorcerer, or one who casts a spell, or a medium, or a spiritist, or one who calls up the dead.
>
> For whoever does these things is detestable to the Lord; and because of these detestable things the Lord your God will drive them out before you. (Deuteronomy 18:10-12)

In Leviticus 20:6, God warns: "As for the person who turns to mediums and to spiritists, . . . I will also set My face against that person and will cut him off from among his people." Judgment is promised again in Malachi 3:5: " 'Then I will draw near to you for judgment; and I will be a swift witness against the sorcerers . . . ' says the Lord of hosts."

The futility of pursuing the occult is told in Isaiah 47: 12:14.

> Stand fast now in your spells
> And in your many sorceries
> With which you have labored from your youth;
> Perhaps you will be able to profit,
> Perhaps you may cause trembling.
> You are wearied with your many counsels,
> Let now the astrologers,
> Those who prophesy by the stars
> Those who predict by the new moons,
> Stand up and save you from what will come upon you.
> Behold, they have become like stubble,
> Fire burns them;
> They cannot deliver themselves from the power of the flame;
> There will be no coal to warm by,
> Nor a fire to sit before!

In the New Testament, witchcraft is listed as one of the works of the flesh in Galatians 5:20, and sorcerers are told in Revelation 21:8 that they will go to hell.

Despite this, witchcraft and occult practices have flourished down through the ages, though mostly "underground" (as described in 1 Samuel 28). Men have been intrigued with the supernatural works of darkness while spurning the supernatural God.

Pagan occult practices date to the ancient civilizations of Babylon and Egypt, and reached their zenith in the Middle Ages. But what flourished in the Middle Ages spread to America and resulted in the infamous witch trials of Salem, has taken on a new face, or rather it has taken on many faces in this so-called "Age of Aquarius."

Let's examine some of these faces.

There are said to be 200 different occults practiced in the world today, from astrology to xylomancy. Of these about seventy-five are practiced in America.

The widespread explosion, exploitation and acceptance of occult practices poses a serious threat to a nation whose traditional heritage and motto has been "In God We Trust."

A survey of today's society indicates that instead of trusting in God, more people are putting their faith in astrology, horoscopes, occult books, Ouija boards, tarot cards, para-psychology, spiritualism, witchcraft, and Satanism than ever before in this country's history.

Here are some figures which indicate the alarming rise in occult interest. It is estimated that at least five million Americans plan their entire lives by the stars, while other millions consult daily horoscopes found in newspapers and astrology magazines. As of April, 1971, some 1,220 of the 1,750 daily newspapers in America carried horoscopes, according to the newspaper trade publication, *Editor and Publisher.*

There is enough business to keep 10,000 full-time and 175,000 part-time astrologers working. An estimated 40 million Americans aided by 10,000 professional astrologers have turned the zodiac following into a $200,000,000 a year business. Currently there are several computers engaged in casting and interpreting horoscopes. One of these prints out a 10,000 word horoscope in minutes for about $20. Another provides horoscopes twenty-four hours a day on about 2,000 campuses in America. A third is located in Grand Central Station in New York City, printing out about 500 horoscopes a day.

The occult has turned into a big business. Hollywood movie stars are among thousands who dial a free horoscope known as "Zodiac Phone."

The Ouija board has been around for a long time. In fact, it was patented in 1892 by Osaac Fuld. After years of sluggish sales, it now sells fantastically well. The Wall Street Journal estimated that 2,000,000 boards were purchased in 1969 alone. It is far more popular than the game of Monopoly made by the same company.

People giving a party can rent a witch through an agency in Cleveland. Sidney Abrams, the agency's organizer, will furnish a witch for between $25 and $200. The witches specialize in tarot card readings, fortune telling, palm reading, or they will conduct séances. They will even furnish a "junior witch" who is only fifteen years old!

Numerous records are on the market in music stores and record stands frequented by young people which deal with "how-to-do-it" witchcraft. The album "Barbara, the Gray Witch" tells listeners whether or not they were born witches or warlocks and also has authentic chants and homage prayers to Satan.

Another recording is "The Satanic Mass" by Anton LaVey, high priest of the Church of Satan in San Francisco, in which he reads from the *Satanic Bible*. I have read portions of his so-called bible. It is blasphemous in the highest degree.

Another record, "The Witchcraft Coven" is promoted as a recording for young people. Its jacket advertises that its aim is to "destroy minds and reap souls."

Occult book sales are booming. They have more than doubled in the past four years. The Library of Congress has more than 800 titles registered, and many occultists have libraries of several thousand books.

Citadel Press, which has about fifteen books on mysticism, reports sales are skyrocketing in college areas, particularly New York, Chicago, Boston, and Southern California.

At public libraries most occult books are always on the check-out list, and many have a long waiting list. Some libraries have had so many occult books stolen that they have discontinued stocking them. At Foothill College Library in Los Altos Hills, California, the entire occult section disappeared!

Occult books have been such a phenomenal success that many respectable publishers print an occult line under one division name while publishing textbooks and Christian books against the occult under other division names.

Ira Levin's *Rosemary's Baby* exploded into a best seller which was later turned into a movie and ranks among the top fifty all-time hits in the motion picture industry. It is the story of a young New York housewife who finds herself trapped by a coven of witches and is forced into a situation which leads to the birth of a child which is half human and half devil.

Jeane Dixon, the Washington, D.C. seeress whose book with Ruth Montgomery, *A Gift of Prophecy*, recounts her accurate predictions while glossing over her many misses, has become a national celebrity. This book has gone through twenty-five paperback printings, selling nearly three million copies. Hardcover sales have reached more than a quarter of a million copies. Mrs. Dixon's autobiography *My Life and Prophecies* is also a big seller.

Life magazine, in a 1971 year-end report on books, indicated that the occult field set the trend. The three books that led *Life* to call that year the "Year of the Demon" were William Blatty's novel *The Exorcist*, Colin Wilson's report on *The Occult*, and *The Occult Revolution* by Richard Woods.

Doubleday's recently created Universe Book Club, which runs ads in many national publications, specializes in occult books only. Since the initiation of this club, the firm has done a booming business. They sell such titles as *Telepathy* by Sybil Leek, *Astrology for the Aquarian Age* by Alexandra Marx, *I Ching* by John Blofeld, *The Encyclopedia of Ancient and Forbidden Knowledge* by Zolar, and *The Encyclopedia of Witchcraft and Demonology* by Russell Hope Robbins.

To entice membership, this club offers four books for ninety-eight cents and a free "Personal Horoscope Handbook." In less than two years the club has reached the 100,000 membership mark.

A San Francisco publisher has produced such unusual best sellers as the *Zodiac Coloring Book*, *Zodiac Cookbook*, *Zodiac Sign-in Book* (autographs), and the *Occult Coloring Book* for children.

The paperback horoscope business, publishing books in a series on signs of the Zodiac, has exploded into a multi-million-dollar business, selling 2,500,000 to 3,000,000 copies each year, according to the *New York Times.* One publisher reports that more than 100,000 gamblers bought "Astrology and Horse Racing" last year.

After decades of decline, spiritualism is again on the rise, probably due to the famous Bishop Pike séances, which I will discuss in a later chapter. There are now at least 400 spiritualist churches in America with more than 150,000 members.

Spiritualism is so popular that the YMCA, noted for its Christian principles, has a full-time spiritualist and healer medium working out of the Washington, D.C. branch.

Rev. Hazel B. Cassell, of the Universal Church of Psychic Science, gives healing messages and performs exorcism there every Sunday and by appointment on weekdays.

The darkest side of the occult, and one that is experiencing alarming popularity, is witchcraft. According to reliable sources within witchcraft itself, there are nearly ten million practicing witches in America. Nearly four million of these are registered at witchcraft centers. The heaviest concentration is in New York and Pennsylvania, but the Los Angeles and Orange County areas of southern California rank near the top of the list.

According to a San Bernardino, California, witch, witchcraft will be the largest religion in the world in the next twenty-four years. In a television interview in San Diego, she claimed that one out of every ten people is now practicing witchcraft, but that only one out of 500 of these would admit it, even to close friends or relatives.

Modern-day witchcraft in the United States takes numerous forms and is spread in a number of ways, from high school classes to television programs.

Witchcraft classes are being taught in many high schools from California to New York under a variety of titles ranging from "Literature of the Supernatural" to "History of the Occult." High school newspapers across the country have been running an increasing number of features on witchcraft, frequently glorifying it.

In interviews with students on campuses in America we found that there is at least one witch on every high school campus. In most schools there are more, sometimes even a coven.

In New York City there are many "witchcraft mediums" who are only twelve or thirteen years old.

Today's rock festivals are frequently described by their young participants and performers as being a "religious experience." "It's like the ego is absolved and you can identify with everyone in the group," one young man said after attending a "Christmas Happening" rock festival in Laguna Beach, California, in 1970.

Observers said that a rock festival at Olympia Stadium in Detroit in October, 1969, showed signs of the new rock merging with the old Sabbat. In fact, Detroit's gathering turned into a Black Arts Festival and was advertised as a gathering of witches. Headlining the Halloween eve event was the rock group known as "The Coven" which reportedly performed the music of a Satanic Mass.

A folk rock musical is credited with a giant boost to astrology through introduction of the song "Aquarius."

Movies, television and radio programs also reflect this growing involvement with the occult, even among programs planned especially for children.

In addition to the bizarre cases of violence listed above, other crimes of destruction, perversion, and murder can be traced to occult involvement.

Rev. Henry Breul of St. Thomas Episcopal Church in Washington, D.C., suspects that the burning of his church last year was the work of a Satanist group and said there was evidence a Black Mass had taken place prior to the burning.

There have been outbreaks of grave robberies both in America and England which authorities blame on witch-craft. In Florida, near Daytona Beach, six skulls disappeared from disinterred caskets. One decapitated corpse was that of the mother of the chief of the Florida Highway Patrol. A cowhorn with a leather thong had been inserted into the neck. Evidence of an occult ceremonial fire was found near another grave.

At a junior high school in California, a young boy was reported to officials for molesting school girls. When the boy's parents were told of this, they were nonchalant. "We are Satan worshipers," they said, "and our son has a demon in him."

Reverend Gordon D. Griffith, rector of St. Clement's Church in Berkeley, was one of a group of Episcopalian leaders who protested the use of Grace Cathedral on Nob Hill for "animalistic symbols and pagan cultic practices" when, during a twenty-four hour vigil at the church, Poet Allen Ginsberg wore a deer mask, and United States senators were named godfathers of animals.

Spiritualists and witches along the Mexican border are charging American parents $40 to protect their soldier sons, some of whom are already dead or reported missing in action.

Evidence of animals being killed ceremonially has been reported by police officials throughout the country. In Venice, California, the chief of police reported that dogs were killed near the beach and their blood drained. There are said to be witch covens in the area which drain animal blood, mix it with LSD, and drink it during occult rites. More than a hundred dogs were found over a period of time in a northern California area with precise incisions made in their skin and their blood drained. Authorities concluded that a communal group was practicing blood sacrifices.

In the same general area, the Charles Manson case brought to light another aspect of the paganism practiced today. Linda Kasabian, a member of the Manson clan, testified during the trial that she believed Manson was a "Messiah come again." A raid on a witchcraft camp in Topanga Canyon near Hollywood revealed a man who claimed to be God.

Dr. Kurt Koch of Germany, one of the leading authorities on the occult who has counseled 20,000 cases and written twenty-seven books on the subject during the past forty years, estimated that in California 40 to 50 percent of those undergoing treatment for various neuroses have dabbled in the occult, and says that most psychiatrists are not aware of this.

California seems to harbor many occultists. Perhaps the most prominent is Anton LaVey, founder of the Church of Satan in San Francisco. LaVey has conducted marriages, baptisms, and funerals in the church, including a "satanic" funeral for a young sailor who had previously been active in an evangelical Baptist Church but who had come under LaVey's influence.

In many areas of the country, LaVey's blasphemous *Satanic Bible* is outselling the *Holy Bible* two to one; and in bookstores near college campuses it has been known to outsell the Bible 100 to one.

One of the most unusual groups on today's occult scene is the Church of Process, based in England, which worships Jehovah, Satan and Lucifer. The 70,000 member group operates out of seven major cities in the United States. Members wear a silver cross for Jesus and a black and red goat-button for Satan.

Man is incurably "religious." He has a definite inner spiritual hunger that continually seeks fulfillment. When he refuses to acknowledge the Lord Jesus Christ, he exposes himself to weird distortions of reality. With disturbing ease, the unbeliever fabricates his own false gods and falls into the snares of the devil.

The secularism of the 1960s has been superseded by a new quest for the spiritual, and initiation into esoteric "in" groups. People will continue to dabble in the occult, with many going on into the dark recesses of the unseen underworld.

All of this paints a very black picture. And without the Lord Jesus Christ the picture *is* black.

But thank God, there is also revival among God's people. Christians across the land are becoming alerted to the sinister forces at work in the world today and have come to the battle!

Succeeding chapters of this book will deal with various areas of today's occult revival as well as pinpointing methods by which we as Christians may counteract this revival and have one of our own—on the Lord's side!

In this book we will walk right into the devil's territory. We intend to expose him for what he is. And we can do this without fear!

People who have made their peace with God through Christ Jesus need not fear the occult. Second Timothy 1:7 declares, "For God has not given us a spirit of timidity, but of *power* and love and discipline."

We have been given the Holy Spirit to empower us, and we have greater power than the devil!

God would not send us into a battle without equipping us. He would not expect us, for example, to go against one of Satan's armored tanks with a water pistol! He would give us heavy artillery, and bombers!

This is what He has done in the spiritual world. He has not sent us against Satan with our own feeble strength, but He has given us the power of His Holy Spirit to equip us for this work! One John 4:4 says, "You are from God, little children, and have overcome them; because *greater is He who is in you* than he who is in the world!"

Thank God He has given us this power, for we surely need it in the age in which we live!

3

Satan's Target: You!

Satan does not confine his aim to any specific age group, or to any precise boundaries, nor to any particular ethnic group. He is not concerned with your age, your sex, your skin tone, nor your IQ.

But he *is* vitally concerned with your *wants*. He can wrap his wildest schemes in trappings which make them appear to be the answer to your deepest desires.

Take the practice of witchcraft.

This is something the ordinary person might associate with old crones on broomsticks with huge warts on their noses and stringy, uncombed hair.

That's not a true picture at all.

The truth is that witchcraft can attract anyone, regardless of educational or financial background or any other grouping.

Here are a few examples encountered during research for this volume.

Robert is twenty, a genius with an IQ of 160 plus. He joined a coven of witches when he was sixteen "just for kicks."

Michael is twenty-two and studying to be a heart surgeon. He once led a Satanic organization because "I was fascinated by the rituals."

Carol is a housewife in San Francisco and her husband is an architect. Every Friday night, they gather eleven other friends at their house for a witchcraft ritual. "It gives us meaning," she says.

John is the twenty-one-year-old son of a prominent senator. He and his friends secretly practice witchcraft.

Glenda is a thirty-five-year-old schoolteacher in Minneapolis. She and a group of her friends meet weekly to explore all facets of the occult, including witchcraft. "It's our form of religion," she says.

Recently when I was on an open-line, live radio question program in Sacramento, a woman called in from the high-class area of Roseville. She was worried about her seventeen-year-old son who was involved in the occult with friends. These boys met twice a week behind locked doors, she said, and committed their souls to the devil.

The list goes on and on—male and female, all ages, from all professions. Witchcraft rolls include doctors, lawyers, writers, school teachers, students, accountants, plumbers, military officers, and even seminary students.

What attracts them to witchcraft?

Many of those involved give varying reasons, but two seem to emerge more prominently than the others.

First, for some the practice seems to satisfy a search for spiritual truth.

Man is basically a spiritual being. When a person does not know Christ, there remains an unsatisfied hunger within his being that starts him on a search for something to fill or satisfy this spirit-craving.

Remember the prodigal son described in the fifteenth chapter of St. Luke? He "was longing to fill his stomach with the pods that the swine were eating . . ." (verse 16), trying to satisfy a human physical hunger with food fit only for a pig.

We have the same picture in the occult: Having spurned the gracious invitation of God and being left with unsatisfied, gnawing hunger in the spiritual man, many turn to substitutes not fit for the lowest animal. Too often the search ends in the occult, where the husks of supernatural experiences seem to offer some type of satisfaction.

Dr. O. S. Guinnes, a British authority on witchcraft, charts "the death of rationalism" as one the motivating forces behind entry into occult practices. People have been "educated" not to believe in God, but still have a hunger for the supernatural, he points out. He also blames modern theology, which has secularized and watered down the Scriptures and explained away the supernatural.

"Reality of the supernatural world has been denied," this scholarly gentleman points out. "And so the last place a person will look for it is in the Christian church, which should believe but does not."

A second strong reason many are attracted to witchcraft is for the sense of individual power it gives them. I have previously noted how Charles Manson and another man involved in the occult claimed to be God or Jesus. The sense of power which many achieve leads them into false identification with the Deity.

In this day and age of big business, big government, big everything, the individual often feels stifled, pushed, or controlled by outside forces.

"I'm just a number," some people say.

"Witchcraft gives me the feeling of power, like I can control my destiny and the destiny of others," claimed one witch. "It give me control I can't get anywhere else because I have access to the secrets of the craft."

A medical student in Florida explained that he got involved in witchcraft to satisfy his need of power. "I always enjoyed dabbling with magic and the occult," he said, "so I went along for the ride. Soon I found myself developing intense hatreds which upset my mental stability. I found occult practices led me to have an intense desire for power. It became a sickness for power, for strength.

"I would try to see how far I could control things—how far I could bend my mind," he continued. "I found the more variance I put into my own brain waves, the more I was altering my consciousness and thought patterns. When I did this, it put me in an extremely unstable position mentally and emotionally. Any mistake, any backfiring, any misdirection would come back and hit you.

23

"I'd say that three out of every twenty young people involved in witchcraft are going to end up in an institution because of it!"

The promise of sex is a powerful magnet held out by Satan to draw the unwary into his power.

Many witches perform their rituals in the nude, claiming that such practice "frees them to release their power." The open nudity, however, is an attractive invitation to further pursuits such as wife swapping, homosexuality, and group sex.

Drug use during witchcraft rituals is another element that attracts young people to participate in the black arts.

Witches and occultists will set up a tremendous protest at this statement, denying that sex or drugs have any part in their ceremonies.

However, interviews with young people across America involved in witchcraft and other occults confirm the fact that marijuana and LSD are frequently a part of the occult scene.

If such open baseness does not appeal to someone, Satan might switch his tactics. He has many.

Perhaps education or mental exercises would work better on someone!

The influence of esoteric Eastern religions has gained momentum in America where there is a tendency to mix any and all beliefs into one big melting pot, often with the high-sounding phrase "It doesn't matter what you believe just so long as you believe something!"

The well-publicized research in psychic and parapsychological fields has motivated people toward the idea that the occult is really a science. Work reportedly being done in psychic research behind the iron curtain has captured the interest of some psychic "scholars."

John. C. Cooper, chairman of the philosophy department at Eastern University, sees the rise of occultism as "a revolt against the scientific and technological rulership of the human mind in the twentieth century."

He echoes the belief that the Western traditional religious institutions have failed to meet the psychic and social needs of Western man.

A witch agreed with Dr. Cooper's statement.

24

"Religion has gotten away from the people," the witch said. "Everyone gets dressed up and goes to church to hear someone else do it. That's not religion. It's one big social club.

"Social club religious services do not give people something to hang on to. They want security. They want to know that a greater power than themselves is with them."

Unfortunately, what these witches have failed to realize is that there *is* a greater power available who will not only be *with* those who desire Him, but will live *in* them.

Jesus, the resurrected, living Son of God, not only has promised His disciples "I will never desert you, nor will I ever forsake you" (Hebrews 13:5), but in referring to the Holy Spirit in John 14:17, He declared, "He abides *with* you and will be *in* you."

There is no greater power that could be with a person or in a person than that! This is what the world needs. This is what it is hungry for! The truth of an ever-present help in the time of trouble is one that needs to be proclaimed loudly in this day and age in which we live.

Unfortunately, that often is not the case.

Associated Press Religion Editor George W. Cornell is another who reports that many who get involved in witchcraft are disenchanted with standard brand churches which give no alternative to the secular world.

Louis Cassels, UPI religion editor, agrees, stating that "In recent years, many theologians have been obsessed with trying to prove to the world that the church is relevant to man's everyday secular concerns through an effort to de-emphasize the supernatural 'other world' aspect of Christian teaching, and to present religion as a here-and-now aid to ethical behavior." This leads many to search for deeper spiritual experiences elsewhere than in the church, Cassels concludes.

People magazine, a Baptist publication, claimed that the move to the occult is the result of the tension of today's world—a retreat to the irrational, where one is relieved of the responsibility of facing up personally to decisions.

"The closer we get to a controlled, totally predictable society, the more man becomes fearful of the consequences," says Mortimer R. Feinberg, a psychology professor at City University of New York. "Interest in mysticism is a regression to a childlike state of mind that relieves man of many of these worries.

"However, many others see the increased interest in the occult mainly as the result of a hoax fostered by those who stand to profit from the fad," Professor Feinberg adds.

Author Arthur Lyons, in his book, *The Second Coming: Satanism in America*, contends that many of those who worship Satan feel themselves unable to come to grips with the social system as it stands. Satanism has made its greatest inroads among the educated upper and middle classes who drift to it because of boredom, he says.

Dr. Henry Pinsker, a New York City psychiatrist, sees many disturbed patients who dabble in the occult. "These are the romantic, the suggestible, and the chronically ill. Every reasonable remedy seemed to fail them, so now they try 'abracadabra,' " he says.

But not all of Satan's bait appears that weighty. He has some hooks baited with "harmless pleasures" and "family entertainment."

Practicing superstition and reading the daily horoscope column in the newspaper may sound harmless on the surface, but both of these, practiced by millions of Americans daily, can be subtle traps to lead into more serious occult practices.

Have you ever turned around to keep a black cat from crossing your path? Or have you gone out of your way to avoid walking under a ladder?

If so, like millions of others, you are practicing a form of witchcraft, though you may not know it. The above mentioned superstitions, as well as many others practiced daily, had their origins in witchcraft.

Here are some other superstitions that had their roots in witchcraft:

1. It was once thought that sneezing meant the soul had temporarily escaped from the body, and the charm "God bless you" was used to keep an evil spirit from taking over the body while it was soulless.

2. Knocking on wood, a common way in which people ward off evil, grew from the thought that wood was a symbol of all the forces of nature. When one knocked on wood, he was trying to bend nature to his will.

26

3. Crossing the fingers is also a custom thought to bring good luck. It grew from the crossed fingers as a symbol of the cross, always a powerful way to ward off evil.

4. The supposition that walking under a ladder meant bad luck grew from the belief that the devil lurked under the ladder leaning against the cross on which Christ was crucified in an attempt to snatch His soul. Although he was foiled in that attempt, he waits under other ladders for other souls.

5. The devil was thought to take the form of a black cat when he roamed the world, and black cats were also thought to be the means by which witches communicated with the spirit world.

6. Carving initials on trees was a practice of witch children who believed once this was done, a couple whose initials were thus carved would be united forever magically.

7. Halloween, the "holiest" day of the witches' calendar, brought about the trick-or-treat celebration because of the fear that if witches were not treated right they would trick their victim with the evil eye.

One of the most subtle magnets to draw people into occult practices is the daily horoscope.

"I can't start the day without reading my horoscope!" I have heard some people say. They may laugh about it, but they are deadly serious.

I even know of one dear old soul, an elderly lady, who had been a member of a fundamental Christian church for years and was leader of a women's missionary group, who wouldn't miss reading her horoscope every morning!

I'm afraid that is true of too many people who could better spend the time in daily devotions, and in seeking God for a good Bible verse to tuck into their hearts to guide them through the day! After all, He says "The steps of a man are established by the Lord . . ." (Psalms 37:23) —not by the stars!

Horoscope readers should give some attention to the blatant inconsistencies and unreliabilities of the horoscope forecasters. The plain fact is that most astrologers disagree among themselves!

To illustrate how inconsistent newspaper astrologers are, my researchers compared on a given date columns by Frances Drake in the *Los Angeles Examiner*; Carroll Righter in the *Los Angeles Times* and *San Diego Union*;

Sydney Omarr in the *San Diego Evening Tribune*, and Jeane Dixon in the *Santa Ana Register*.

On the first date compared, only one similarity existed for any one sign, and that was when Scorpios were advised of "fine opportunities" by both Carroll Righter and Frances Drake. Most of the columns gave entirely diverse readings.

Here are a few of the outright contradictions:

Virgos were told by Righter to entertain at home in the evening, but were advised by Omarr to attend the theater.

Leos were told that they were in the doldrums by Righter, who advised planning recreational activities as a remedy. On the same date, however, Leos were told by Omarr that they possessed an abundance of optimism.

Libras were told by Miss Drake that they could plan their day pretty much to their liking, but Mrs. Dixon did not agree. She said their personal plans might get a temporary setback.

Aquarians were advised by Miss Drake to shape their finest plans and follow through consistently. Omarr's advice was to "lie low . . . there is no need to rush, push or cajole."

Pisces were told by Miss Drake to execute a decisive program, and by Mrs. Dixon that they would see their temporary reverses in perspective.

The "Star Gazer" column which runs in the *San Bernardino Sun Telegram* is a column in which you select your horoscope on a code number basis. The readings are very general. For example, Aries might be told that their "judgment is apt to be more accurate," while Virgos are advised to be "wary of wrong food or beverages." Meanwhile, Pisces are noncommittally warned to express "views that cannot give offense."

Comparisons on other dates also showed few similarities. Contradictions included advice given to those born under the sign of Cancer where one columnist said "hold off on journeys" and another advised them "to go places."

Virgos also received diverse advice. "Make all decisions thoughtfully" and "ride with the tide" by two of the forecasters; another two disagreed on another point, telling the Virgos that "you are dynamic now and can make an excellent impression on others and gain favor" or that "today demonstrates again that business and pleasure mix very poorly."

Capricorns could take their choice, or try to assimilate all for views on one particular day, if they craved mass confusion! They were counseled to (1) Be flexible in your thinking, (2) Let caution be your keynote, (3) You want to expand and can do so, and (4) If you're going to do something, get into it and do it all at once.

Pisces were told both that some of their ideals might be cast aside, and diversely, that they should speak up for their convictions.

Many Hollywood movie stars employ high-priced astrologers to chart their days, reflecting the general instability and lack of religious faith exhibited by many of the film colony's residents.

They, and other millions of believers in astrology, are ignorant of a fact that would make the entire situation humorous, if the end result were not so tragic.

It is this: in theory horoscopes are prepared by believers in the system, using ancient knowledge about the positions of stars and planets in the zodiac. However, astrology has not accepted the Copernican theory; it continues to base its prognostications on the faulty idea that the stars, sun, and planets revolve around the earth!

Whatever the reasons that people become involved in the occult, Paul saw it coming long ago, when under the inspiration of the Holy Spirit he wrote, in 1 Timothy 4:1, "But the Spirit explicitly says that in later times some will fall away from the faith, paying attention to deceitful spirits and doctrines of demons." This prophecy has certainly been fulfilled in the occult scene!

John Phillips, a reporter writing in the *New York Times*, warned, "Satan is at work today in the world and in the United States with an intensity unmatched and experienced. . . . Whether we like it or not, wearing blinders will not help. Americans desperately need to know what the Bible says about it before tragedy strikes homes and families who do not know what is happening to young members or why."

I couldn't agree more! And I urge *you*, the reader, to *saturate* yourself in the Word of God, to put on the whole armor of God! (Ephesians 6:11) For in today's battle for souls, you and your children are the target!

But be of good cheer! God is able to deliver you and keep you! Ephesians 6:10-13 says:

> Finally, be strong in the Lord, and in the strength of His might. Put on the full armor of God, that you may be able to stand firm against the schemes of the devil. For our struggle is not against flesh and blood, but against the rulers, against the powers, against the world-forces of this darkness, against the spiritual forces of wickedness in the heavenly places.
>
> Therefore take up the whole armor of God, that you may be able to resist in the evil day, and having done everything, to stand firm.

4

Hollywood
Leads the Parade!

"From Hollywood, the entertainment capital of the world, comes—*witchcraft!*"

For years Hollywood has been the pacesetter in the rapid decline of America's morals, glorifying illicit sex, expounding the case for permissiveness, and blessing the frequent changing of marriage partners.

In the amazing witchcraft revival sweeping America, once again the glamorous entertainment area not only has been thoroughly involved, but must be credited with leading the parade! With its long arm of influence, it has swept through theatres and homes, via the television tube, to fan the flames of interest in the occult throughout the nation.

We have already mentioned *Rosemary's Baby* which quickly grossed more than $40,000,000 and ranks among the top fifty all-time hits of the motion picture industry. Anton LaVey, high priest of the Church of Satan, was appropriately chosen to portray the devil in this film, which he describes as "the best paid commercial for Satanism since the Inquisition."

He may be right, for a survey by Dr. Arnold Wilson disclosed that many people now involved in witchcraft had their interest aroused by that particular film.

Who knows how many others were influenced by such films as "The Devils," a show so distasteful that even most reviewers condemned it? A *Los Angeles Times* review labeled it as "truly degenerate and despicable" while the *Saturday Review of Literature* summed it up as "morbid mis Miasma . . . wanton violence . . . shameful carnality." *Playboy Magazine* called it "one of the most vulgar films ever made" and *Newsweek* declared that "it might have been written and filmed by Nero and the Marquis de Sade."

Yet even this film found a champion. In the *New York Times* a reviewer cited "The Devils" as "an ambitious work, a visionary work, a prophetic warning."

That particular film was rated "X," but many of the films depicting Satanism and witchcraft carry merely a "GP" rating, permitting them to extend their lures to audiences of all ages.

"The Brotherhood of Satan" is an example. This film has the added attraction of offering each moviegoer a packet of "Seeds of Satan's Soul" with instructions on how to plant the seeds in order to gain protection from "the black magic of the Brotherhood of Satan."

Unlike such standard horror films as "Frankenstein" and "Dracula" where the monsters are eventually destroyed to eliminate evil, this film ends with the triumph of Satan and his worshipers.

The potential spiritual effect on children by negating the age-old principle that "good will win" is shocking, but the greatest outrage in conjunction with this film was the circulation of materials in the schools of Youngstown, Ohio, advocating membership in the Church of Satan!

Other occult movies which have been attracting large audiences, particularly among the young, are "Simon—King of the Witches," about a man with strange occult powers; "Brotherhood of the Bell," about idol worship and murder; "Crow Haven Farm," in which witches seek revenge; "The Satan Spectrum" which shows a cripple and deaf mute being sacrificed to the devil, and many others.

People actually involved in the occult filled many of the roles as actors in these films or gave technical assistance to make the occult rites authentic.

This could also be "the decade of the occult" in television, where such popular programs as "Bewitched" and "I Dream of Jeanie" give rise to America's benevolent acceptance of "good" witches.

The TV lineup now includes "Sabrina the Teenage Witch," "The Sixth Sense," "What's Your Sign?" and other series with occult themes as well as single episodes in many major series which deal with the occult.

In the children's viewing realm, it is nearly impossible to find programs without occult overtones. Even Sesame Street has its Wanda the Witch, while most current cartoons depict witches, goblins, ghosts, and other eerie beings.

Television and radio producers seem to ignore a provision in the National Association of Broadcasters Code which calls for disclaimers in programs relating to the occult, particularly astrology. The code calls for informing the viewer that the program is "for entertainment purposes only and that the stars do not in any way control or influence man's actions."

The key statement in the code on occult programming is that "Exhibitions of fortunetelling, occultism, astrology, phrenology, palm reading, and numerology are acceptable only when required by a plot or the theme of a program, and the presentation then should be developed in a manner designed not to foster superstition or to excite interest or belief in these subjects."

The code also prohibits advertising which "promotes the practice of astrology, fortunetelling, occultism, phrenology, palm reading and similar subjects." Despite this, many advertisements have occult themes and many occult programs carry no disclaimers.

The code is very clear, and if more people would take issue with local stations and network shows, it would be possible to curtail some of the shows.

Another entertainment form making its presence felt in the occult field is folk-rock music,

The stage show "Hair" led the way in boosting astrology with its highly popular song "Aquarius." More than sixty million people have seen this musical despite its onstage nudity.

Other musical entertainments have joined the bandwagon, such as the 1969 Detroit rock festival which was advertised as a gathering of witches.

Just as at the ancient sabbats, today's rock concerts feature widespread use of hallucinogenic drugs, throbbing, hypnotic music, and orgiastic dancing.

We have also mentioned some of the popular albums which have spurred interest in the occult. In addition to "The Grey Witch" offering and LaVey's "Satanic Mass," "The Witch Queen of New Orleans" promotes voodoo and has been high on pop record charts.

"The Black Mass" by the Witchcraft Coven not only gives music but includes complete instructions for performing a Black Mass. "It is as authentic as hundreds of hours of research in every known source can make it," the album cover advises. "We do not recommend its use by anyone who has not thoroughly studied black magic and is aware of the risks and dangers involved."

Nor has the family game been omitted from Satan's list of occult weaponry in the field of entertainment.

The toy shelves of department stores are full of such occult offerings as "Magic 8-Ball Fortune Teller," "Genuine Vampire Kit," "Voice of the Mummy," "Madam Planchette," "Which Witch?" and "Barnabas Calling."

Best known, of course, is the Ouija Board, for which Parker Brothers purchased the rights in 1967. It quickly surpassed their longtime favorite game, Monopoly, in total sales.

Although the owners avoid claiming that the Ouija can foretell the future, they have sent out a free pamphlet on "the weird and wonderful world of Ouija" which recommends a booklet entitled "How to Develop Your ESP Power," by Jane Roberts.

This booklet, in turn, refers to a long communication by use of a Ouija Board between the author and a deceased man.

What makes the little planchette move across the Ouija Board to answer questions for the curious?

This is how the Ouija process was described in the patent application: "A question is asked and by the involuntary muscular actions of the players, or through some other agency, the frame will commence to move across the table."

"Some other agency" is the explanation preferred by spiritualists who insisted that "forces from the great beyond" move the planchette to communicate messages from the dead.

Many people have related to me weird tales of answers given by the Ouija Board. This and other occult games may seem intriguing, but the implications are serious and are not to be tampered with. They can lead to dangerous waters indeed. Use of a Ouija has even led to violence and murder, such as a case in Arkansas where a teenage girl shot her father. She told investigators she had received her instructions from the Ouija Board. I think that cases such as this more than remove the Ouija from the "game" designation!

While we are discussing the influence of witchcraft on entertainment and vice versa, let us take a look at still another field which has felt this influence—the innocent-appearing comic strip.

"Little Orphan Annie" has long had her "Asp" with strange powers, and "Mandrake the Magician" is an oldie which has passed away.

But the new line-up includes "Dark Shadows," "The Wizard of Id," and "Hazel the Witch" for home consumption.

A major airlines recently offered a free cartoon book entitled "The Little Devil" to child passengers. Invariably, the "Little Devil" was victor in every situation presented in the comic book story.

A single cartoon is often used on barbecue aprons or greeting cards to depict what has become a very popular statement: "The devil made me do it!" Although no doubt meant to be amusing, the humor of the slogan is lost on those of us who realize its terrible, stark reality. Here is another clue that the hand of Satan is delving into every phase of today's entertainment world to win recognition and honor for himself.

5

Classroom Invasion

A satanic Black Mass celebrated right on the campus of an American high school? Unthinkable! Or is it when you consider the course our nation's public schools have taken just in the last decade or so?

Don Carpenter, writing in the Montrose, California, *Ledger* of June 9, 1971, declared, "When prayer was eliminated from the schools, it was a compromise. When Satan replaced God, it was a surrender."

This writer then pinpointed a growing public concern over the revolution which has rocked our public schools from all levels: kindergarten up to higher education.

The public school system of America, remember, was once founded on the Word of God. Years ago *Pilgrim's Progress* was a standard textbook. Without traveling that many years back, many can remember when "The Lord's Prayer" was recited during home room period, or when the teacher could select a portion of Scripture for devotional reading.

Those days are gone, due largely to the efforts of atheist Madalyn Murray O'Hair and Supreme Court rulings regarding prayer and the Bible in public school.

What is transpiring today in the schools will shock

many parents, for Satan is meeting with surprisingly little resistance as he attempts to use the classroom to capture the minds and imagination of our young people.

Courses in the occult abound in many schools, and actual witchcraft rites have been reported in some classrooms. Experimental college courses are being funded by tax money, and in some cases known witches are teachers.

Though witchcraft purports to be a religion, there is no hue and cry about separation of religion and public education where the occult is involved as there was over the Christian religion.

However, not every community is taking this onslaught of the enemy without a battle. Residents of the California city of Fresno took concerted action to pressure the school board into dropping courses in the occult from the curriculum after they discovered what was happening in the local classrooms.

Their success in the battle should be an inspiration to leaders in other communities to take up the standard to combat this growing spiritual menace.

Fresno is a good example of how Satan infiltrates the schools, and also a good example of how a community can defeat this type of activity.

On the surface, the community appears to be a pleasant, progressive city which is facing up to the challenges of the future. It has high-rise buildings and modern shopping centers, two newspapers, two colleges and several dozen churches.

But drive around Fresno and you find some disquieting reflections of the times.

On Blackstone Avenue is one of three shops in town which sells pornography. Two blocks from Fresno City College is a bookstore which deals in literature of the occult and the black arts. Near Fresno State College is another bookstore where the owner says he cannot keep up with the demand for a popular item, the *Satanic Bible*.

Talk to Fresno residents, and after you find out all the good things about the city, conversation turns to discussion of bombings of public buildings. Concern is expressed over the existence of the pornography bookshops and the influence they have on young people and the city's "all-American" image. You also find people who are concerned with drug abuse and the soaring venereal disease rate.

People also are disturbed over the schools—about what is being taught, and about where their tax dollar is going.

Apparently the first infiltration into the schools was made at Fresno State College, where a course entitled "Mysticism" was introduced in 1968. This was taught by Dr. George Kauffman, a professor of chemistry with unimpeachable credentials in the field of chemistry.

His credits include work experience with Humble Oil and General Electric companies, a teaching assignment at the University of Texas, and participation in research at the Oak Ridge National Laboratory. Also he has traveled to the Soviet Union where he presented papers at the International Congress of the History of Science. With this background it seems a waste that he would be assigned to teach in the occult field.

For five semesters the course attracted no special attention, although it dealt with mysticism, Satanism, witchcraft, and magic.

Then a routine press release was issued by the college news bureau regarding the appearance on campus of John A. Ferro, whose topic was to be "Satanism and the Dark Side of Life."

Following are some quotes from the news release.

"His talk is sponsored by the Form Arts Committee of the College Union, and he will be the guest of Dr. George B. Kauffman, an instructor in the college's course in mysticism. Ferro will also spend time in seminars and discussions with Dr. Kauffman's class on Satanism, witchcraft and magic. . . . Ferro is a student of Crist Lovdjieff and worked with Anton Szandor LaVey, high priest of the Church of Satan in San Francisco."

The press release also said Ferro would emphasize the carnal aspect of man's nature as well as the functional value of satanic personification. Satanism would be discussed as a philosophy of revolt and emancipation.

"The lecture is open to the public," the release continued, "and the day chosen for Ferro's appearance is

'Walpurgisnacht' or the eve of May Day in which witches traditionally ride to an appointed rendezvous."

Murray Norris, alert editor of the prize-winning *Fresno Guide*, sent an observer to this particular "rendezvous" in the person of Father Cecil Barron of St. Anthony Claret Catholic Church.

Father Barron had spent fifteen years in England where he had witnessed the practice of Satanism. He was especially interested in Ferro's talk since the Catholic Church is one of the prime targets of Satanists, whose Black Mass mocks the Catholic Mass.

At the lecture, Ferro boldly stated that "the core of Satanism is that it is a philosophy of revolt. There is far more in Satanism about revolt than anything else."

Father Barron's report declared that Ferro "attacks all the known moral standards of society as well as all religious tenets. He degrades man to the level of an animal. He urges man to become a god unto himself. Satanism destroys the whole structure of society because the licentiousness of it is beyond comprehension. Satanism is out to destroy everything decent."

The priest also questioned whether the "teaching of Satanism at Fresno State was a proper use of our tax monies."

Residents made suddenly aware of the presence of Satanism in their city fired off a barrage of indignant letters to the editor.

"Just who wouldn't be angry . . . our tax money being spent for such an ungodly and ridiculous course?" demanded one writer, who signed the letter with the slogan "Prayer Changes Things."

But reaction to the college course was mild compared to what happened when it was revealed that a course in witchcraft was being taught in the local high school.

Entitled "Literature of the Supernatural," these high school courses were credited by bookstore owners with triggering an interest in the occult that sent sales zooming on books dealing with black magic, witchcraft, and devil worship.

"I don't know how deep they go into it in class," one

bookstore owner said, "but they certainly get these kids interested in witchcraft and worship."

While some school officials denied that students were being actively indoctrinated in witchcraft, young people nonetheless were exposed to courses which taught them how to become witches or warlocks; how to perform a Black Mass; how to cast a horoscope; how to tell fortunes; how to read tarot cards; how to document psychic experiences; how to conduct a séance, and other practices in violation of God's laws, city and state codes, and the United States Constitution.

Father Barron again became a spokesman for opponents to the classes, condemning any course which taught witchcraft to young people.

"This is the height of infamy," he declared. "Witchcraft is a part of devil worship. They're all connected . . . witchcraft, black magic, and devil worship. They may seem like something to play with when they cover these things in class, but they are getting close to things that pertain to Satanism.

"The *Bible* condemns witchcraft and says that they that do such things shall not inherit the Kingdom of God" (Galatians 5:21), he pointed out further.

The high school pilot course had been requested by a teacher named Edna Eisentrager in a communication to Edison High School Principal William Gillen. The new course was needed, Mrs. Eisentrager's request form stated, because "students have shown an avid interest in supernatural literature."

In a standard form requiring information as to bibliography for the course, the following paperbacks were listed: *The October Country* by Ray Bradbury; *Witches, Warlocks and Werewolves*, edited by Rod Sterling.

She said the subject would not require specially trained teachers; there were informed people already available.

Initiated as an elective in the English Department, the course was divided into areas covering psychology, vampirism, lycanthropy (werewolves and other changelings), spiritualism, monsters, witchcraft (sorcery, magic, and voodoo), divination (necromancy, augury, and astrology), and study of *The October Country* (modern supernatural).

"The reasons why man has developed fears of the unknown, and the forms these fears have taken, will be highlighted to help the student examine his own fears and superstitions." This was part of the study, according to Mrs. Eisenstager's written plan.

Books originally requested for the course were by well-known authors, many that parents would not find objectionable. But in reality nearly 100 hardcore occult books were used as primary resources instead of the books mentioned in the original requisition for the course.

The new course opened at Edison High School with 150 students enrolled in five classes taught by Mrs. Eisenstrager. The next year the course was introduced at Hoover High with an enrollment of 120 students and at Roosevelt with 46 students.

Students interviewed said they took the courses because they could make an "easy" *A* or *B*.

Requirements for a passing grade were listed as follows: "Read at least four books, and study one particular area in depth so that you can perform a demonstration for the class or give an oral report in which you tell what you have learned and your conclusions with the reasons why you feel as you do (belief, disbelief, skepticism, etc.) or submit a written report to the teacher."

This course was clearly dabbling in the area of beliefs and was challenged before the school board by Miss Marilyn Affeldt, a *Bible* saleswoman.

"The matter of beliefs is not an English subject, nor is it a subject for any school teaching," argued Miss Affeldt before the Fresno School Board. "It is clear that this is not an English course. It just happens to be written in English. This is, instead, a course dealing with beliefs, and this is illegal, just as any doctrinal or religious course would be illegal."

Miss Affeldt researched the State Education Code for ammunition for her board appearance and found that the definition for "Literature of the Supernatural" was at odds with the state mandate for high school English courses. She also found that federal money was being used to subsidize the occult courses in some situations.

42

Citing specific portions of the Federal Education Act of 1965, Miss Affeldt declared, "The English elective courses being presented in our Fresno High Schools are clearly outside the intent of that act." She charged that so-called "enriching" courses had been substituted for mandatory ones.

Requirements for getting an *A* in the course were spine-tingling! For this requirement a student was required: "Read at least six books and study one particular area in depth. Join with at least three other members of the class who are studying in your same area and meet with them at least twice each week for group discussion or experiments. Prepare an original individual or group discussion or presentation for the teacher and the class: a bulletin board display, or a piece of supernatural fiction in poems or short story or play, *or a séance*, or *fortune telling demonstration* using various methods, or a supernatural creation using media other than language (sculpture, painting, movie), or a group presentation of a supernatural play, or rewrite a true incident or a short story in a play form, etc., *or teach at least four people individually or in groups: I Ching, how to read the tarot cards, the art of astrology, palmistry, etc., or chart a horoscope for at least four people (including the teacher) or study J. B. Rhine's clinical experiments for ESP and set up a laboratory situation in which you test at least ten people for ESP powers and write up the results of your tests, or study Dal Lea's methods for documenting psychic experiences and describe, document, and present a written report on at least five psychic experiences.*"

The combined bibliography from two Fresno high schools for "Literature of the Supernatural" included 100 hardcore occult books, including such titles as *Diary of a Witch* and *Book of Fortune Telling* by Florida witch Sybil Leek; *The World Within* by Gina Cerminara, which deals with reincarnation for solving personal problems; *Dreams— Your Magic Mirror* by Elsie Sechrist, which promotes dream interpretations; *The Betty Book* by Stewart White, said to be "revelations from the unseen side of life;" *The Door to the Future* by Jess Stearn, which says that the future can be predicted through psychics; *Practical Mysticism* by Evelyn Underhill, a learn-how book of using mysticism;

The Haunted Mind by Dr. Nandor Fodor, which advocates levitation and astral projection; *True Experiences in Communication with the Dead* by Martin Ebon, which promotes spiritism; *Astrology, the Space Age Science* by Joseph Goodavage, which attempts to add credibility to astrological predictions; *I Ching—Book of Changes* by Wilke Wilhelm, which tells how to practice the occult; and *Enigma of Out-of-Body Travel* by Susy Smith, which deals with astral projection.

What benefits did the students taking the course derive from it?

One student who took the course in the spring semester of 1971 picked werewolves as his project.

"I read some material on werewolves and talked about it in class. This did not help my English in any way. It really didn't help at all. The only thing I could say was that it might have helped my public speaking, but I was taking a public speaking class anyway. I took the class because I didn't know what other class to take. I talked to other kids, and I figured it would probably be easy. They offered classes in composition, but they were too hard, or over my head. But what I really needed was a class in basic English . . . something that would help my spelling.

"In the classroom, there were books like *Man, Myth and Magic*, the *Satanic Bible* and *The Black Arts*, a big formula dictionary on witchcraft which contained things about incantations.

"The teacher said she had gotten in trouble teaching the course in the past. So we all had to have a special project. Some girls the quarter before had gotten her in trouble when they put on a Black Mass demonstration. She didn't want anything like this to happen again," the student said.

The Black Mass to which he referred took place on a Friday the 13th at Hoover High School. Details of the mass are sparse. Students would not talk about it.

Another student described a class in "Literature of the Supernatural" in which a student speaker discussed the "world of astral projection."

"He said one of the ways to get into the astral world was to take drugs, but that this would destroy your body.

So he said you should get there by concentration. He said he could talk to the dead and that he had the power to see other lives he had lived in reincarnation. He claimed he was reincarnated as an Eskimo and as other people in past lives."

The student also described a séance held in class.

"It took in about thirty people. We left the classroom and went into this soundproof room at Hoover. A black candle was lit, and we tried to contact this kid's uncle. The teacher wasn't in the room, but she let us go to the séance.

"One student got up in class and said his mother was a witch. She had been practicing since she was a girl, and she only considered herself an amateur. He told about books that had certain marks in them put there by other witches and said if anyone tried to use the book, something drastic would happen to them—like an accident or something. He also said that when his father died, a group of witches came to his house and sat around a table, and his father's voice came through one of the women. It was weird!"

Many students who were exposed to the "Literature of the Supernatural" felt they had been misled and deprived of correct English instruction.

"I didn't get anything out of it. It was just a big waste of time for an easy grade," one boy said.

"What bothers me," confided one girl who is a devout Christian, "is how much students seemed to look forward to playing occult games as soon as they were out of the classroom. There's no telling what a lot of kids have gotten into as a result of the ideas they got in the course."

It was through the Fresno newspaper that the parents and other concerned citizens of that community first became aware of what was happening in their schools, and Editor Norris is to be commended for the fight he led to rid the community of that blight.

When the story was revealed in the *Fresno Guide*, public reaction was almost unanimously against the course.

"If you can teach Satanism and witchcraft in the schools," one woman said in a letter to the editor, "why can't we have God and prayer back in the schools?"

45

The school board heard about the taxpayers' anger through the great number of protest letters which flooded the newspaper office. Threats of recall against the board were heard, and suggestions of taxpayer marches.

But the greatest resource the community had was prayer—the spiritual battle done in a number of Fresno churches. Dozens of prayer groups met morning, noon, and night to pray against the continuance of occult courses fostered upon the children of the community. Included were housewives, businessmen, blue collar workers, and farmers.

Nor were the prayer bands limited to what are normally called "fundamentalists." They included members of every denomination in Fresno, Catholic, Protestant, and Jewish.

"There must be 500 people in Fresno who meet regularly for prayer and Bible study," Norris reported. "Don't underestimate the power of prayer. It does work. It worked in Fresno."

After a two-hour hearing in which some eleven persons spoke out against the course, the Fresno Board of Education and school administrators announced that they had arrived earlier at a decision to drop the course, "Literature of the Supernatural," from the coming year's curriculum. This was at least a temporary victory for Fresno citizens.

School Superintendent Dr. Arnold E. Finch was quoted in the *Fresno Bee* as saying: "It has not been the practice of the district to continue to offer elective courses whenever there is a sizable misunderstanding and misinterpretation of the content or intent of the course."

Misunderstanding? Misinterpretation?

The high school courses were not reassigned for the following year, nor did Dr. Kauffman's course on mysticism open on the Fresno State campus. However, it was offered at the "Experimental College" under the title of "Alchemy," still taught by Dr. Kauffman.

Fresno is not alone in its fight against occult courses in public schools.

My researchers discovered that half of the public schools contacted are teaching occultism! This is done under deceptive course titles or through campus lecture series where off-campus speakers come and advocate occult involvement.

San Diego State College is funding an experimental

46

college course in witchcraft taught by an admitted witch, said also to be a member of the Gay Liberation League. Also in the San Diego area, an occult course is being taught for seventh graders at Hale Junior High School.

"It was the most signed-up for elective," according to the teacher of the class who was given the teaching assignment from administrators even though he said he preferred not to teach the subject.

At San Francisco State, although "Magic Myths of Medicine" relating to voodoo was discontinued, a new course was started entitled "Mystic of Metaphysics."

San Francisco has occultism in the junior high schools where a "mini course" is taught in English classes.

A summer extension course entitled "Mystical and Scientific Basis of Divination" was given at UCLA.

At Oglethorpe College in Atlanta, 190 students are enrolled in five classes on the occult with a waiting list of 500 for the next session. The teacher is Anita Josey who claims that she is psychic.

Regarding the phenomenal interest in her classes, Miss Josey said, "This is just a drop in the bucket compared to what is going to happen all across the country. This is just the beginning."

The popularity of occult courses continues at various high schools around the nation. The "Literature of the Supernatural" course has been offered in Sanger High School and a similar course entitled "Magic, Myths and Science" was taught at Lodi High School, both in California. In Minneapolis at South and Washburn High Schools, 172 students are taking the course under the title "The Occult."

Courses have sparked other types of occult interest including the formation of the Samohi Occult Club at Santa Monica High School in California. Club members sell knickknacks on campus to raise money to buy supplies for their practices.

The Denver Free University requires a $10.90 surcharge for its course on "Theory and Practice of Witchcraft." The extra fee is said to cover the cost of candles, bats, blood, and other items needed for the class.

It might be interesting to note that when community pressure is applied to occult practices as a whole, those involved begin to claim that witchcraft is a religion and demand their "religious rights" under the first amendment to the Constitution.

If we accept their own definition of witchcraft as a religion, then why is this "religion" permitted in schools where Christian activities are not condoned?

And why is it taught where Bible classes are banned?

It would seem that the abolishment of public prayers and other religious activities in tax-supported schools applied only to the Christian religion.

Witchcraft or any other occult being taught in public schools should be opposed vigorously because of the non-academic value and the serious problems to which such studies lead, such as demon possession, unstable personalities, mental derangement, criminal tendencies, and possible self-destruction—a road easily traced in our occult files.

Also, the need for legislation in this area is clear. If witchcraft should be defined as a religion by lawmakers, then it should be excluded from public schools as Christianity is.

However, legislation itself is not the answer to the crisis in America. This is part of the revelation insight into the spirit world that God gave me—which led to the production of this book.

God revealed to me that we are not dealing with men, nor with political ideologies, nor with hippies, nor with drugs, nor with horoscopes, but with spirits and principalities, and the forces of the enemy.

He also revealed to me the answer.

He said to me, "Son, the answer cannot be legislated from Washington, D.C. As long as you try to meet these forces with a solution from man, you are wasting your time."

There is only one way to stop what is happening to our kids today.

That's when you and I break through in the spirit world, get hold of those principalities and those demons and those spirits which are controlling and dominating and driving the lives of these kids, bind them in the name of Jesus and cast them out!

6

The Devil's Advocate

Satan's quest for respectability and academic acceptance didn't pause at the high school or state college level.

A milestone of sorts was reached on June 16, 1970, when a large, well-known university bestowed a Bachelor of Arts Degree in Magic upon Phillip Emmons Isaac Bonewits, a one-time disciple of the Church of Satan described as a "social misfit" by a former teacher.

The degree was signed by Governor Ronald Reagan and administrators of the University of California at Berkeley.

"A bit weird" by his own summation, the diminutive 107-pound Bonewits roams the streets of Berkeley attired in a medieval red satin outfit with a large sword on his belt. Armed with his university credentials, he has opened a "Wizard Consulting Service" in Berkeley.

California has more than its share of "different" people or "characters," so many in fact that such places as Sunset Strip in Hollywood and Telegraph Street in Berkeley have become tourist attractions just to "see the people."

Our purpose here is not to single out one person for his strange costume or unconventional behavior, but to question the action of school administrators in engaging in such academic frippery as to give a degree in the subject of "Magic," and, in effect, grant a license for the man to practice sorcery.

Bonewits may be considered a "joke" by some, but the situation certainly should be taken seriously when public institutions of learning lend their considerable prestige to such undertakings. Here is a clearly unscriptural field of study being endorsed.

That the practice of sorcery *is* unscriptural is clear from such passages as Deuteronomy 18:10-12, a reference mentioned earlier, which says:

> There shall not be found among you anyone who makes his son or his daughter to pass through the fire, one who uses divination, one who practices witchcraft, one who interprets omens, or a sorcerer, or one who casts a spell, or a medium or a spiritist, or one who calls up the dead. For whoever does these things is detestable to the Lord; and because of these detestable things the Lord your God will drive them out from before you.

Bonewits has written his own definition of magic which differs considerably from that of Webster. According to Bonewits, magic is "a science and an art comprising a system of concepts and methods for the buildup of human emotion, altering the electro-chemical balance of the metabolism, using associational techniques and devices to concentrate and focus this emotional energy, thus modulating the energy broadcast by the human body, usually to affect other energy patterns whether animate or inanimate, but occasionally to affect the personal energy pattern. Magic is a way to control psi-phenomena."

I'm afraid I would need a new college degree myself to figure that one out!

Several people who knew Bonewits at San Clemente High School were interviewed so that we could get a more accurate picture of the world's first sorcerer with a university degree.

"I almost fell dead when I heard that Phil had gotten that degree from Berkeley," said one person, now working in Florida. "I didn't think he would get anywhere. But he must have done something right. He was just a weird person in high school, and you know how kids can be in high school. He was comical, almost a Jerry Lewis-type person, uncoordinated, doing things that were just out of the ordinary. He was just the type of person to try anything and make it look ridiculous because he knew it would.

"He actually looked ridiculous because of his proportions and ideals. He was a negative person—an opposite type. He liked to argue for the sake of an argument. But he would never admit to being a loser. If it looked like he was going downhill and was going to be the loser, he'd laugh it off and walk away.

"He dressed very weird. One day he would wear an old professor's type outfit—baggy tweed sport coat, blue shirt buttoned all the way to the top, baggy trousers. Next day he would come in with real tight pants and a flowery shirt with billowed arms. He just liked to be different.

"He graduated from high school a year early and everything he did was *A* work. He went wholeheartedly into his work.

"He kissed a school girl one time. She screamed and almost fainted. This was one of the high school pranks. He walked into the student store and gave this girl a big kiss. She almost turned green and ran out of the store. He really wasn't the most popular boy on campus."

The teacher who termed Bonewits a "social misfit" added, "He was a genius, no doubt about it. But he did the minimum work possible to get through."

In late 1971, Bonewits was arrested by Berkeley police for brandishing a sword at another Berkeley man. He drew a stern lecture from a judge who took the weapon from him.

When Bonewits first arrived in Berkeley, he spent much time in mocking Christian street evangelists.

"I'd always been interested in theology and metaphysics, and I was rather disgusted by the low quality arguments being offered," he declared. "But I also noticed that all the standard techniques of heckling and such were totally useless. So one day I got a small microphone and a small amplifying set and came out with a routine I called 'The Devil's Advocate!'

"I knew all of the evangelistic techniques inside and out, all of the preaching arguments, all of the games they could play. So I did them. There would be a row of seven or eight people and there I would be right in the middle, preaching Satanism right on the street corner!"

It was at this time that Bonewits got involved with the Church of Satan. He said that a woman came up to him one day while he was preaching and said she was a witch with Anton LaVey's Church of Satan in San Francisco.

Bonewits met LaVey and was impressed by his extensive library of occult books. He went to the weekly Friday night services, even serving as an altar boy at the Black Mass, he said. He eventually dropped out of this group as he had from others.

"I've been into almost every major religious mainstream in the United States," Bonewits says. "I've spent several months at a time intensively reading the Scriptures or being a member of different groups.

"I have participated in services with Catholics, all different flavors of Protestants, Hindus, Moslems, Jews, various and sundry little nut groups like we have running around the Bay area, including the Satanists, which I suppose comes under the heading of Christian.

"I don't last long in them. They usually kick me out fairly quickly.

"I'm into witchcraft to a certain extent. I consider myself a pagan these days because I find I can get more out of the old nature religions than I can ever get out of any of the modern religions.

"There is the problem of separating the field of witchcraft and formal scholastic magic; sometimes I'm acting as a magician, and sometimes I act as a witch. It depends on what sort of ritual I'm doing and in what context.

"I'm not a pacifist, but I do believe in keeping violence down to a minimum. If somebody wants me to kill someone who's upsetting them, I normally find that just making them sick or making them go away through casting a spell is much more efficient than bothering to kill them. Breaking a guy's leg or blinding him will do the job. There's no sense in using your sword to kill him.

"There's always going to be a little bit of violence because we're a violent species. But if you can keep witchcraft violence to a minimum, you'll find it's a much healthier atmosphere for people to live in," he declares.

How Bonewits acquired his degree reflects the changing and permissive attitudes in higher education today.

Instead of structured courses of study in a general area such as economics, sociology, anthropology or communications, the new university allows the student to draw up his own area of study.

Bonewits was interested in a great number of subject areas but apparently could not stand the discipline of perservering in any one area.

"In high school, I was considered a bit weird, but also a genius. Unfortunately, none of the people were able to decide what I was a genius at," he is quoted as saying. "I was glad to get out of high school, into college, and then into the university where I could use a four-letter word without everybody freaking out over it," he declared.

When Bonewits arrived at the Berkeley campus in 1968, he says he was "thinking of psychology" as a major, and also of communications. "But I was also interested in extra sensory communication, telepathy, and such. After a while I did not care if I got a degree or not.

"So I just started grabbing courses from anthropology, psychology, sociology, rhetoric, drama, linguistics, oriental religion, folklore, mythology, and others. I took the courses that interested me at any one particular time, including some non-credit courses in astrology, tarot cards, etc."

He says that it suddenly dawned on him that he had enough credits for an individual major, so he persuaded Professor Nelson H. Grayburn of the anthropology department to be his sponsor.

Two weeks later the College of Letters and Sciences Deans' Conference met and decided to approve Bonewits' major.

Thus, on June 16, 1970, the Regents of the University of California, on the nomination of the faculty of the College of Letters and Science, conferred upon Phillip Emmons Isaac Bonewits the degree of bachelor of art with a major in magic, "with all the rights and privileges thereto pertaining," given at Berkeley.

With his diploma signed by Chancellor Roger Heyns,

Charles Hitch, president, W. D. Knight, dean of the college and California Governor Ronald Reagan, Bonewits has been given license to venture forth in life, preying on the gullible and spiritually weak.

The implications arising from this self-styled "Wizard's Degree" should be of deep concern to every taxpayer as well as every Christian. That a great university would stoop to such academic frivolity is hard to believe, according to one university professor. It is also a waste of taxpayers' money.

The Bonewits degree, however, is a clear indication of the set of the sail in today's world: Berkeley now has an entire department in witchcraft, and Bonewits, who has had one book published and is planning to work on a doctorate in magic at Stanford, has boldly declared, "Today Berkeley, tomorrow the world!"

7

Counterattack!

I cannot see all these things happening in America without doing something about it.

I don't intend to stand idly by and see this spirit of occultism, this spirit of anti-God sweep through our nation and engulf our young people without doing everything I know how.

Thank God for what He has shown me of the battle in the spiritual world and how to have authority over the powers of Satan.

God has given me a worldwide ministry in which I could keep busy all the time, holding crusades and conferences around the world and training national ministers by the thousands to continue the work in those foreign fields.

But that's not enough. The things which God has shown me about the condition of America today and what caused that condition are for a reason.

I have already found out how to take on Satan, actually invade his territory, in my own life. Since I have discovered these secrets, I am seeing the back side of Satan as never before. He's on the run, and he is going to keep running.

James 4:7 says, "Submit therefore to God. Resist the devil and he will flee from you."

I have a desire and a burden to share what I have learned with others so that they too may experience continuing victory in their own lives.

One way of sharing this is through this book. There are also two other tools which God has enabled us to prepare in our all-out counterattack.

In January of 1972, I unveiled the world's first anti-occult mobile unit, which has been highly publicized throughout the United States and Canada.

Newspapers, radio, television, and the general public have all found this Witchmobile very interesting. However, it is meant for more than entertainment, and it is also meant to be more than merely educational on the natural level.

I want it to be an eye opener to people about what they can get into and what it can do to them. I also want it to be inspirational so that it will motivate them in a positive way.

To make this unit authentic, the fields of the occult were highly researched for months.

The Witchmobile is colorfully painted to show the "pretty" mask being stripped off Satan to reveal the true ugliness underneath. That is what we have done, presented the ugliness underneath the bait that traps the unwary.

Inside the unit are hundreds of occult items, including a real human skull and a robed satanic priest. The seemingly "pretty" side is depicted by meditation lamps, beads, etc., as well as the more horrible appearing details.

The purpose is to warn young people how even innocent-appearing items may lead eventually to the degradation of Satan worship.

Each visitor to the unit is given a free copy of another highly researched tool which is being effectively used in this counterattack. This is the special edition of *Up-Look*, the youth publication of Morris Cerullo World Evangelism, entitled "What's Wrong with the Occult?" More than 175,000 copies of the colorful twenty-page tabloid were distributed by churches, other organizations and individuals during the first seven months it was in print, and is still being ordered in huge bundles by interested organizations. You may write for a free copy. Simply address a postcard to: Morris Cerullo, P.O. Box 700, San Diego, California 92138.

We have also had a tremendous number of requests from individuals and organizations for the Witchmobile to visit their areas, which indicates the tremendous public interest that has been generated.

The mobile unit has been in use in Southern California in conjunction with Action Center, the youth outreach program of the Morris Cerullo World Evangelism ministry in San Diego. "Occult stop" programs and "dope stop" seminars have been conducted in many schools and churches and will continue.

The mobile unit is now being taken throughout the nation to point millions of souls out of darkness into the light of Jesus Christ.

In putting this authentic display together, we ran into one aspect of this occult revival in America which we had not realized before. That is, that this is big business! This is no penny ante stuff. Somebody is making money—big money—out of the witchcraft upsurge.

The unwitting public is victimized as semisecret occult ordering houses charge highly inflated prices for what often amounts to mere trinkets.

It is estimated that the public spends more than two billion dollars a year on occult items, and many of these items are virtually worthless. Scores of occult mailing houses are doing business throughout America on an unprecedented scale—peddling Satan!

Recently in San Francisco I passed an occult supply house that does $25,000 a month in sales. They have such a booming business that they can't keep some items in stock.

In doing our purchasing, we found that in voodoo products, the buyer usually gets taken twice—first on the high cost of the items and secondly on the fact that what is sent is not exactly what is advertised in the catalog.

For example, the Voodoo-Jinx-Removing-Bag for "neutralizing curses" sells for $3.50. It is hard to describe the worthless junk contained in the little four-inch-deep pouch.

There's a small nail, a paper pentagram, a small yellow birthday candle, a little yellow feather, two bobby pins, fragments of cork and coal, a fragile snake ring, a cheap puzzle, a plastic fingernail, something that looks like a miniature plastic claw, and a tiki charm "made in Hong Kong."

We also found that voodoo charms have been modernized. Now many spells are contained in aerosol spray cans and can be sprayed around! These include "Fortune Teller Spray," for use in séances; "Jinx Removing Spray," for which instructions state "use this spray with convictions;" and "Gold-Silver Spray," to use in "your place of business."

Then there is the "Double-Fast-Luck Spray," with which one should "spray often for this reward;" "Love Spray," with instructions to "try your love with it," and "Gambler's Spray," which tells the user to "spray this at all times before you start any game of chance. This spray may change vibrations for you."

Judging by the odor of some of the sprays, the only thing they might do is kill cockroaches, but they will cost the buyer three dollars a can.

If you don't care for the sprays, you can get the same items in bars of soap or in jars of shampoos for one dollar.

Other voodoo items available include a Black Cat Eye for $2.50; a Swallow's Eye for $5, or graveyard dust for $2. Those ordering the graveyard dust may specify whether they want the dust to be taken from the grave of a suicide, an unbaptized infant, or a murder victim.

For use in spiritism séances, one can purchase an aluminum trumpet "imported from England" for $17.50. This turns out to be a sheet of thin metal rolled into a twenty-inch cone which could be duplicated easily for less than one dollar.

A tinny, cross-hilted sword used in Satan worship retails for $25. It would cost the tourist $5 in Spain where it is made. A hooded black robe which contains not more than several dollars worth of cheap muslin retails for $35.

A wispy black wand less than two feet long sells for $5. A white wand, which turned out to be a two-foot length of quarter-inch dowel, sold for $1. A bat skull is priced at $22.50 and a cat skull at $17.50. The price of a rattle-snake fang is $2.25.

One firm specializes in "genuine human skulls" for $100, and advertises that it can "supply a very large selection of skeletons or their parts in most instances—human, animal, lizards, snakes, and bats. Send us your requirements and we will quote a price."

One of the big areas of the occult business boom is in occult books where most distributors offer several books in the one dollar range, presumably to get persons started in the occult. Some of these include *Do It Yourself Witchcraft Guide, Complete Book of Witchcraft, Cannibal Cookbook,* and *Spell Rituals.*

Occultists already hooked pay higher prices for the "heavier" books such as *Treatise on Cosmic Light,* $10.50; *Egyptian Religion of Resurrection,* $15, and *A to Z Horoscope Maker,* $12.

One of the businesses contacted during our research was the Llewellyn Publishing Company, located in an old redstone mansion in Minneapolis. Both Llewellyn and the Gnostica Bookstore across the city, are operated by Carl Wescheke, bearded forty-one-year-old bachelor whose interest in the occult and publishing has catapulted him into one of the kingmakers of the occult business. The purple and white bookstore building is also used as a school where the curriculum includes occult subjects from astrology to witchcraft.

Wescheke says business is good.

A review of some of Llewellyn's publications is guaranteed to startle the uninitiated in the occult. Among the titles offered are *Fertility Chart, Mastering Witchcraft,* and *Zen Macrobiotic Cooking.* Personal services offered include *Natal Chart and Astrology Book,* $19.95; *Fertility Cycle* for one year, $5, and *One Question Answered,* $10.

For $2.95 you can buy your own "Gemini Scan Kit." The ad claims that "as soon as you open this complete astrology kit, you can start compiling personal horoscopes."

Among the items which may be purchased in addition to books are Aura Goggles, $35. That may sound like a buy when you find out a list of contents in each kit! It includes Standard Aura Goggles, fitted with normal aura filters; spare goggle frames for use with extra filters; set of six pairs of complementary color filters for use on inner aura or in psychological conditioning; set of three pairs of graded aura filters to aid progressive development of outer aura vision; pair of inner aura filters, methylene blue, sensitized for development of inner aura examination; and a pair of extra dark aura filters, for those who need extra color complementary effects for aura vision."

Suppliers are usually secretive about their business, including the actual location of their offices in many cases. But the operator of Tyrad mail order house in Minneapolis did reveal something about markups and profits.

"The markup on a $100 skull is minute," said the owner. "They're so high-priced that they're outrageous. It costs me $90 wholesale for a skull, and I resell at $100. That's not much profit for the trouble of handling that order.

"You've got to have five to seven times the wholesale price markup on an item to make out. We really make out on jewelry, though. The higher priced the jewelry, the higher the markup," the man said.

Books and candles are the biggest occult supply sellers, followed by general items such as crystal balls, witches' robes, and jewelry.

Many of these items are in our Witchmobile as well as are all sorts of mixes for magic potions, occult "games," items used in spiritualist séances and Eastern meditations, displays dealing with Hare Krishna and Mexican voodoo, various skulls and bones, musical albums with their bizarre jackets, and a variety of occult books, including one on how to concoct hexes.

Highlighting the display is a hooded mannequin, depicting a witch, with authentic altar items before him: chalice, dagger, goat's foot candle holder, fire pot. About his neck hangs one of the most bloodcurdling items in the exhibit—an upside-down cross containing the numerals "666," the number of the Antichrist described in the book of Revelation.

It was not pleasant working on such a display. It meant handling items for which the instinct was to draw away. It meant facing some realities that many Christians or others of high morals would rather shun, but which are on display in stores and shops today before the eyes of our young people.

We have brought them together for one purpose: not to glorify the devil, but to expose him. We are not using these instruments for worshiping Satan, but we are using them to show that Satan can have *no* power over the man, woman, boy, or girl who will put his trust in the Lord Jesus Christ.

The items put into the unit are a good indication of the worth of anything Satan has to offer! The items are costly—but they are really cheap, tinny things.

The real cost of the occult, however, is not the dollars and cents which are paid for potions and books. The real price is in the toll of human lives, the suffering and heartbreak, the cost in souls. That's the great price often paid for a bunch of tinsel, trash which cannot satisfy.

I am reminded of the verse in Isaiah 52:3 which says, "You were sold for nothing. . . ." I'm glad that is not all of that verse; however, for it continues, "You will be redeemed without money."

That which is of real value cannot be purchased with money. True value can be found only in Christ. Without money, using the currency of His own blood, He has made the way for young people trapped in the occult, or in any other evil snare, to be reconciled with God.

> . . . You who have no money come, buy and eat.
> Come, buy wine and milk
> Without money and without cost.
> Why do you spend money for what is not bread,
> And your wages for what does not satisfy?
> Listen carefully to Me, and eat what is good,
> And delight yourself in abundance.
> Incline your ear and come to Me.
> Listen, that you may live. (Isaiah 55:1-3)

"For God so loved the world, that He gave His only begotten Son, that whoever believes in Him should not perish, but have eternal life." (John 3:16)

8

Death and Destruction

Have you ever sat down at camp and watched insects trying to get at the fire of your gas lantern? They beat and flap against the glass globe, trying to get to the pretty flame inside, never realizing what will happen if they do.

The next morning, the lantern will contain a large number of dead insects who have somehow managed to find their way inside and have been killed by the deadly flames they thought were so attractive.

Every time I hear of young people playing with the things of Satan by participating in fortune telling or séances or meditation trips, I want to warn them against the very flame which is attracting them, for in the end it will defile and destroy.

My files are full of examples of the most grotesque violence you can imagine which has been brought about by occult involvement. Many violent crimes have resulted from experimentation in satanic practices. These instances are horrifyingly frequent.

Playing with the occult is similar to playing with fire, only tragically more serious a hundred times over!

Some may edge close to the fire and then retreat when it gets a little warm without being badly burned.

Others might become involved more seriously and get burned when they realize the demonic forces at work. They might escape, but not without permanent scars on their lives and in their minds.

Another, disregarding all warnings, might walk directly into the fiery hell of the occult realm and never return. These are the ones who, trapped and deluded by evil spirits, turn to killing or self-destruction. They bring tragedy and heartbreak to their families and friends, and often they experience a violent end themselves.

We often hear that the "Age of Aquarius" in which we live is the age of "love and understanding," but we had better stop and think again when we hear some of the grim stories of murder and suicide associated with the occult. We had better pause and ask ourselves what is really happening today.

The plain truth is that there is no love nor understanding among the people who wander into the dark abyss of witchcraft and black magic. The scene, instead, is set with hatred, with jealousy, and with perversion.

Often friends and relatives take the whole matter lightly when someone begins to dabble in the occult. Sometimes they even laugh when signs of interest are shown.

Our case histories include that of a young man who was known as "a joker," but who died a horrible death through experimentation with the occult.

According to friends, this young man was persuaded that if he died a violent death, he would join Satan and become a leader of forty legions of demons. In his delusion, he convinced two of his friends to help him kill himself. Now he is dead and they are in prison.

This young man's mother reported that the youth was "always kidding" about witchcraft. Now she and his friends know it was really no laughing matter at all.

How did twenty-year-old Patrick Michael Newell of Vineland, New Jersey, get led so far down the occult path that he met this tragic and useless death?

At Vineland High School, he was known as an average student with an above average interest in history and mythology.

Mike and his three sisters lived with their divorced

mother in a farmhouse on the outskirts of town. A younger brother lived with his father and an older brother was serving in the United States Marines.

A hint of Mike's interest in the occult is given in his high school yearbook, which says that Mike enjoyed "collecting ancient spells."

Unlike most teenage boys, Mike had no interest in learning to drive and was driven to and from his job at the Dueer Glass Company in Vineland by his mother.

Two of Mike's best friends were Richard Williams, two years younger than Mike, and Carl Sweikert, three years younger. Richard and Mike had been arrested on a petty theft charge when they were younger. Both Williams and Sweikert were star runners on the cross-country team.

Neighbors described Williams as understanding and polite. They said Sweikert gave a "little boy" impression. All three boys were regarded as "nice average kids." What happened on the night of June 15, 1971, was not average.

On this night the three boys attended a graduation party at the home of a friend.

"Mike was joking and laughing with everyone," one girl recalled. About 10 P.M. the three boys left the party, climbed into Sweikert's car and drove to Millville, a small New Jersey residential community. Turning off onto a dirt road, they drove through a thick forest of underbrush to a large pond known locally as a sand wash. The pond was an excavation originally made by glass manufacturing companies and later filled with water. It had become a popular swimming place on warm summer days.

But a cooling swim was not Mike's plan this night.

He got out a roll of wide adhesive tape that Sweikert used to tape his feet when running cross country and asked his friends to bind his hands and feet. According to their later testimony, Mike begged them, "Please do it. Nobody knows what you guys know. As my best friends, you should help me."

After the boys bound him they helped him into the water.

"We took him out two steps and he sat down in the water of the pond and laid his head back," one of the boys told police later. "He started making noises like 'go.'"

"He lay down and put his head back and took a big mouthful of water and swallowed it," Sweikert told police. "Then he just lay there and kind of hunched his shoulders, and he said, 'Go.' He started making these weird sounds, and his eyes were becoming glassy too. He just looked like he put himself in some kind of a coma or trance of something."

"We guided him out in the water—he floated out and just sank. He didn't say a word. When the bubbles came up, we waited. Nothing happened, so we went back to the car and left and went back to Vineland," Williams told police.

The body was discovered three days later by other boys swimming in the pond.

Questioned by police, Williams and Sweikert admitted being with Newell, and the story of the deceased youth's involvement with witchcraft and self-destruction began to unfold.

"One night we were over at Mike's house," Williams told police. "We [two other boys, Williams, and Newell] were sitting there. We were going to sleep when all of a sudden, Mike got up. It was midnight. He walked forward to the light. There was a sword hanging over the top of the mirror. He took the sword off the top of the mirror and ripped the buttons off his shirt. He had all this red ink on the sword and all kinds of designs or lettering on it that I had seen in some of his witchcraft books.

"He looked at us real weird and shut off the lights. He screamed. He just missed [hitting] one of the kids [with the sword] by about half an inch. Then he just turned the lights back on and walked over to the bed. He didn't even look at us. Then he went to sleep.

"He was always talking about sacrificing a live person, getting him and tying him down," Williams said.

Sweikert told police that while the three were out on a camping trip one time, Newell got up at midnight and started wandering around and uttering some kind of chant.

On another occasion, according to a youth who claimed to have attended a ceremony led by Newell, "He had a triangular chart on a piece of paper that he put down on the floor inside a circle. In the corners of the triangle he placed fake animal skulls with candles burning inside them.

"Then from a small case he took two hamsters. He held one in each hand and said an incantation. He screamed as loud as he could and squashed the hamsters with his hands. One moment they were squealing. The next moment they were dead. He rubbed the blood on his arms and gave a closing incantation."

Newell also was reported to have immolated hamsters by shaking them in a box studded with nails. Such a device was found by police among Newell's possessions.

The young men gave other illustrations of the death and destruction which had been on young Newell's mind. They said he had offered them money to kill his brother and other people as well as himself.

On the night in question, they said Mike insisted that he had to die.

"He said he would never forgive us if we didn't go through with it," Williams told police. He said Newell told him he had made him beneficiary of a life insurance policy in exchange for his services.

"He said he felt Satan needed him," Williams said.

Some townspeople still refused to believe that there was witchcraft practiced in Vineland, but several ministers viewed Newell's death with concern.

One of these was Rev. Harry Snook, pastor of the Chestnut Assembly of God Church in Vineland. He estimated that sixty or seventy people of high school age had been involved as spectators or participants in satanic worship rites.

He said he got his information from former drug users who attended "rap sessions" at his church. He said he spoke to a number of young people who had taken part in witchcraft and devil worship, although none had any connection with Michael Newell.

Rev. Joseph Donchez of the First Presbyterian Church, who has also worked with young people with drug habits, agreed with Rev. Snook, although he gave a higher estimate of the number of youth involved.

The subject of witchcraft and Satanism is no longer

a joke in Vineland. In fact, many people who knew Mike are reluctant to discuss it at all.

A girl who said she knew Mike well told a researcher, "Nobody wants to talk about it. Everybody's scared to say anything. They say they don't want to get involved. But how can I not be involved?"

Williams and Sweikert were sentenced to up to ten years in prison for their part in Newell's death.

This particular case is not the only one in our files which dramatically illustrates the tragedy which can result from involvement in witchcraft.

Another example is the death of James Michael Schlosser, twenty-two, a Great Falls, Montana, social worker. Schlosser was described by a friend as a "kindly person, always doing favors."

One of these favors was giving a ride to a hitchhiker, a youth also twenty-two years old, named Stanley Dean Baker. This boy, hitchhiking near Yellowstone National Park, was described by friends as a "friendly boy who changed from a crew cut boy scout into a long-haired hippie."

Schlosser was killed at a secluded spot for no apparent reason. His headless, limbless torso was later found floating in the Yellowstone River.

Several days after the death, Schlosser's missing auto was involved in a hit-and-run accident in Monterey County, and this accident eventually led to the arrest of Baker and a companion named Harry Allen Stroup.

The next part of the story isn't pretty. Both Baker and Stroup had parts of human fingers in their pockets when they were arrested!

While being questioned, Baker blurted out to the officer, "I have this problem. I'm a cannibal!"

He admitted to being involved in occult practices such as witchcraft. A *Satanic Bible* was in his possession.

He confessed to officers that he had cut off Schlosser's head, arms, and legs—and that he had eaten Schlosser's heart!

One of the investigators in this case was Salinas County Detective Sergeant John McMahon. "In my twenty years of police work," he said, "I have never had an investigation that made me so nauseated."

Baker has been sentenced to life in prison for this killing.

Here again research painted a "nice-average-kid" picture of Baker. He had gone with his father on hunting and fishing trips in the Big Horn Mountains at an early age. He had a reputation at school as a friendly boy and an average student. He was interested in football and in basketball.

He won the "God and Country Award" for his boy scout activities, and for years he served as an altar boy in the Catholic Church. He wrote an impressive letter nominating his dad for Sheridan's "Father of the Year" award and won.

What went wrong? How did a happy, respected kid end in the shape he did? What sparked his interest in the occult? Friends may forget some of the good things about his early life, but I doubt if anyone who knew him will ever forget the gruesome details of his satanic activities that put him where he is today.

We have another case in our files where palmistry was evidently the interest that got a young businessman "hooked" on the occult. It led to a double murder and suicide in October of 1971.

This man was Mallory Giffe, Jr., thirty-five-year-old real estate operator in Nashville, Tennessee.

He and a friend kidnapped Giffe's twenty-five-year-old estranged wife Susan and tried to hijack a private plane to the Bahamas. The trip ended tragically in Jacksonville, Florida, with the pilot, Susan and Giffe all dead, apparently by Giffe's hand.

The occult role in this needless slaughter is easy to trace.

Here was a man who had been a respected businessman in his community. He headed a real estate firm known as the Global V. Realty. He was in the sand and gravel business in Marietta, Georgia, and was about to become part owner in a nightclub called La Bri in the black area of Nashville.

La Bri was owned by Bobby Wayne Wallace, forty-two, the friend who assisted in the kidnaping and hijacking.

Wallace was later charged by the FBI with kidnaping and by the state of Florida for murder.

Giffe had also been a biology professor at one of the universities in Nashville before he began these business ventures—and then got into the occult.

Friends said that Giffe's interest started with palmistry after he was once told that he had "the devil's palm." According to Reporter Wendell Rawls of the Nashville Tennessean, who did an in-depth story on the case, this "meant he was very lucky."

"Every friend that I talked to said the outstanding characteristic of Giffe was his interest in palm reading and the occult," Rawls reported. Giffe claimed he had supernatural power and that his grandmother was a witch.

One couple told Rawls that they came for dinner one night and found Giffe wearing ceremonial robes and sitting in the middle of the living room floor with incense and a candle burning in front of him. He had a picture of Mrs. Giffe and a former boyfriend bordered in black crepe paper.

"He'd be chanting some kind of gobbledegook over the picture, endeavoring to place some kind of hex over the former boyfriend," Rawls said.

Rawls also discovered Giffe liked to eat anise seeds "because it was supposed to be the food for warlocks."

Once again a relatively mild interest in the occult led to violence and death. The case should serve as a deterrent to others who feel drawn to such activities as palm reading, astrology, and other occult practices.

There are other criminal cases still under investigation at this writing in which the occult, witchcraft, and ESP are involved.

In Oregon, a newspaper carried a story with the headline "YOUTH DIES EXPLORING MYSTERIES OF ESP." The story starts out that "An apparent exercise in extra-sensory perception took the life of an eighteen-year-old youth whose body was found in a garbage can."

A book on ESP found among the boy's effects had an underlined passage that said "a person must experience pain before being able to receive messages."

This case was still under investigation by Oregon State Police.

In Albuquerque, New Mexico, the possibility loomed that witchcraft might be involved in the defense of a woman charged with the murder of her husband.

Parents and friends of victims and suspects involved in tragedies such as the ones we have mentioned still find it hard to believe that participation in the occult had anything to do with the crimes.

However, more and more often the role of the occult in violent crimes is being brought to light. In many cases, police are slow to recognize or use the occult connection in preparing and prosecuting cases.

The trend is changing, however, and in Tustin, California, officers serving under Fred Krasco, head of the narcotics division of the police department, have been instructed to watch for clues dealing with the occult.

If friends and relatives are alerted to some of these clues, they may be able to help prevent tragedies such as the ones I have related here.

Black candles, a Satanic Bible, pictures of the devil's pentagram, a talisman or amulet, or black or white robes are some of the things that can point to a person's involvement in the occult. Voodoo dolls, a taste for occult books, an upside-down cross, a goat's head on clothes or in jewelry, or a "goat's head" salute are other telltale signs.

We have in our files a newspaper photo of a northern California woman charged with the stabbing of a teacher. She is plainly making the satanic salute in this photo although the article accompanying the picture makes no mention of it. This salute is a common greeting among witches.

An abundance of slain animals may indicate the presence of witchcraft since small animals often end up in satanic rites, and the possession of human bones may be part of the eerie trail left by Satanism.

A reliable police source has stated that in California during the past three years, more than 100 murders have had some kind of occult involvement indicated. Information gathered from police records shows that people practicing any type of occult may be involved in violent crimes.

Figure 1 is a "scoreboard" prepared from police and newspaper files to indicate the wide scope of violent crimes in which indication of occult activities has been bared.

71

CASE	CRIMES	LOCATION	OCCULT INVOLVEMENT
Edward Paisnel	Assault, rape, and sodomy with children	England (Island of Jersey)	Black magic
Dean Baker	Murder of a social worker	Great Falls, Montana	Church of Satan
John Frazier	Murders of five people	Redwood City, California	Tarot Cards
Zodiac Killer	Murders of 13 to 17 victims	California	Astrology
Steven Hurd	Murder of gas station attendant and school teacher	El Toro, California	Church of Satan
Kim Brown	Murder of a sixty-two-year-old pensioner	Miami, Florida	Witchcraft, Satanism
George Giffe	Suicide after murdering two in plane hijacking	Jacksonville, Florida	Palmistry, Witchcraft Reincarnation
Rose Hardy	Classroom stabbing of two teachers	San Francisco, California	Meditations, Satanism
Charles Manson	Murder of seven people	Hollywood, California	Astral Projection, Satanism, Thought Transfer
Leroy Olinger	Suicide (Age 18)	Oregon City, Oregon	ESP
Sharon Tate	Victim of occult murder	Hollywood, California	Witchcraft, Church of Satan
Beatrice Gardner	Murder of her husband	Albuquerque, New Mexico	Witchcraft
Mike Newell	Suicide (Age 20)	Vineland, New Jersey	Oriental Mysticism, Witchcraft

There is another scoreboard also being kept, but the names there may never make the headlines; thank God for that. Included in these are the growing number who are being delivered every day out of the occult—by the power of God.

In my American crusades, we usually have one night in each city in which we stress deliverance from various kinds of bondage. There have been thousands of folks delivered from many different things. Some are freed from the use of alcohol or tobacco after years and years of enslavement.

We've seen the "sixty-second heroin cure" work on hundreds of kids throughout the nation. This happens when hard-core addicts are completely delivered by the power of God, without experiencing any withdrawal symptoms.

Thank God occultists can also experience a sixty-second cure, once a commitment is made, and they turn to God in earnest. That's often all the time it takes to make the difference between whether they are entered on the scoreboard of violence such as quoted above, or whether they are written in the annals of Heaven after being delivered from the bondage of Satan.

The sample of violence I have presented is grim, but who knows how much grimmer it would be except for the grace of God which permits thousands to be rescued before it is too late.

9

The Manson "Messiah"

One of the most gory and most publicized crimes connected with occultism concerns Charles Manson and his "family." In this case seven people and an unborn baby were slaughtered in a two-day killing spree.

Manson was the "father" of the clan and looked upon as the Messiah by some of his followers. In fact, he was so deep into the occult that at times he really fancied himself to be "Jesus, the visible manifestation of God." At other times he claimed to be the devil. Certainly Satan's influence is to be found in this story, certainly one of the most sensational mass murders in history.

It made headlines around the world when actress Sharon Tate, three of her friends, and a passerby were slain the night of August 9, 1969. The other victims were Voyteck Frykowski; Jay Sebring, a men's hair stylist; Abigail Folger, the coffee heiress, and an eighteen-year-old boy who had been visiting the caretaker.

Miss Tate, an expectant mother, was the wife of movie producer-director Roman Polanski, who was in Europe at the time. The bloody horror scene which shook the nation took place at the Polanski's rented home in Hollywood Hills.

Two days later, a couple was found stabbed to death in similar fashion in their Hollywood home.

For months the Los Angeles Police Department sifted through stacks of theories and clues. Eventually, a suspect arrested in Texas confided details of the crimes to a cellmate, and the case broke. Police arrested Manson and members of his family of runaway girls and young men who had been living on an abandoned ranch outside of Los Angeles.

"When you talk about me," Manson told reporters after his arrest, "make me a tough guy, the meanest man in the world. Make me the devil."

Two writers, John Gilmore and Ron Kenner, who wrote the book *The Garbage People* did paint a pretty ugly picture of Charlie. After interviews with him in the Los Angeles County jail, they compiled a description which included this description: "He contorts his body with the control of a fakir—into a shape not human. His skeleton seems rubbery, unbreakable, and mystifying. The eyeballs seem sucked inward and the insistent outline of his skull is right there. You are shocked. He is a monster."

Although Manson was not present at the Tate murders, which were executed by Charles "Tex" Watson, Susan Atkins, Leslie Van Houten, and Patricia Krenwinkel, he and three of his followers were sentenced to death for the murders. Later the Supreme Court ruled the death sentence to be unconstitutional, and Manson and his convicted clan members are now remaining in prison.

The seemingly senseless killings raised countless questions in the minds of people around the country. Many people played detective in trying to answer questions about the slayings, but one area was almost overlooked completely. Though not explored by the press nor advanced in depth at the lengthy trial, it was learned that the occult had played a curious and continuing role in the lives of both Charles Manson and victim Sharon Tate.

Charles Manson's deep interest in the occult was evidenced while he was serving time at McNeil Island Prison on several charges, including forgery and passing bad checks. Here he began studying magic, warlockery, hypnotism, astral projection, and Masonic lore, according to authorities.

When he was released in June of 1967, he headed for San Francisco's Haight-Ashbury scene where there were thousands of flower children, dropouts, and lost souls seeking subcultural expression in drugs, acid rock, sexual freedom, long hair, communes, guerrilla theatre, underground newspapers, astrology, tarot cards, and all forms of the occult.

To those who remember Manson in San Francisco, he was what one person describes as "a glib, grubby little man with a guitar scrounging for young girls using mysticism and guru babble, a time-honored tactic on the Haight."

Manson became a familiar figure among the flower children. He boasted about hanging around with the Diggers as they distributed their daily food in Panhandle Park. Some people believe he may have stayed in a house on Waller Street which was later renamed the "Devil House."

Besides a haven for peace-seeking, peace-loving hippies and runaways, Haight-Ashbury became a magnet for motorcyclists, rapists, long-haired criminals, and Satanists.

Manson was moving in and out of the different crowds, attracting girls with his hypnotic techniques. Among those drawn to him were some girls who, when they lived across the Bay in Mendocino, were known as the Witches of Mendocino.

When Manson had assembled a faithful group of followers, including the Witches of Mendocino, he acquired a bus which was painted black, and the group made their way south to Los Angeles. A popular gathering place for hippies and dropouts in those days was the once glamorous Sunset Strip along Sunset Boulevard.

Motorcycle groups with satanic names like The Satan Slaves, The Straight Satans, and Jokers out of Hell were a part of the Sunset scene, and there Manson made contact with them.

To this day, many of the girls who followed Manson still wear the satanic motorcycle gang jackets along with shaved heads and X's carved on their foreheads above the eyes in imitation of their "master."

As Manson's "family" grew it took on the characteristics of the motorcycle clubs with its outlaw attitudes, male chauvinism, obsession with "death trips," rituals, and

Satanism. New girls in the "family" wore ownership ankle chains like many girls in cycle clubs.

The family's proclivity for violence and the occult may have come from a satanic motorcylce club, The Satan Slaves, whose members lived and operated in the Malibu-Topanga Canyon areas. Some members wore medallions which they purchased at an occult shop in Hollywood.

Four members of one particular motorcycle club were supposedly linked with an obscure satanic cult of some forty members called the Circe Order of Dog Blood, according to Ed Sanders, a reporter who spent two years researching Manson and his family for his book called *The Family*. The Circe group, according to Sanders, held outdoor ceremonies twice a month on new and full moon nights on secluded beaches of Los Angeles and Ventura counties. According to police, they sacrificed black dogs, black cats, roosters, and probably goats. Other elements of voodoo were present in their rituals, including belief in werewolves.

Manson's family and the cycle club were close friends, and observers agree that his association with the Circe group had a great influence on Manson's thinking.

Manson was also known as a "knife freak," and investigators learned that he gave his female followers lessons in knife throwing, at one point instructing them on throat slitting and skull boiling.

Manson borrowed and perverted ideas and practices from many sources to the point that many of his female followers continue to believe that Manson is Christ and the devil in one.

Anyone who was around Manson could attest to his ability to quote the Bible at great length, twisting Scripture to his own use.

In fact, Manson twisted the minds of his followers so far that the girls who once maintained a twenty-four-hour-a-day vigil for him outside the Los Angeles County Jail claimed that "Charlie is the devil—Charlie is Christ."

The basis of this odd duality on Manson's part is obscure, although some observers note similarity with the beliefs of the black-caped members of the Process Church of the Final Judgment which arrived on the Los Angeles scene in early 1968. Members of the Process Church worship Jehovah, Lucifer, and Satan.

While the Process Church denies any connection with Manson prior to his arrest, they published a long, wordy statement by Manson in a 1972 "Death Issue" of their magazine.

Charles Manson's associations with the macabre evil forces of Satan were clearly established before the murders. Borrowing from the occult and any number of other sources, including the Bible, he mesmerized his followers into obeying his every command, including the one to kill.

Meanwhile Sharon Tate and her friends were reportedly carrying on their own kind of amusement. There was much talk in Hollywood about Sharon's involvement in the occult. To what extent she dabbled with occult practices is not clear. However, there are few doubts about the report that while making her first major film, *Eye of the Devil*, the movie company hired an English magician named Alex Saunders, the so-called "King of the Witches," as technical adviser.

Saunders, also known as the High Priest Verbius, claims to have initiated and trained people in 200 covens of witches in the British Isles. He claimed that he became a friend of Sharon Tate on the set of the devil movie in London, and before filming ended, he allegedly claimed that he had initiated Miss Tate into witchcraft.

Phillip Bonewits, a former altar boy in Anton LaVey's Church of Satan, stated in an interview that Sharon Tate was a member of the San Francisco-based Satan worship organization.

Sharon Tate married the Polish born Polanski in 1969. Polanski has a reputation for liking to produce dramatic, far-out films. A number of his films, notably *Knife in the Water, Cul-de-Sac*, and *Repulsion* have achieved great success. We have already noted that *Rosemary's Baby*, which Polanski directed, has been a great box-office hit and is a classic of occultism.

There are stories that real-life Satanists and adherents to evil were angered with Polanski for making *Rosemary's Baby*, and that Sharon's death was a revenge slaying. To

79

what extent that theory is true, like many other facets of this case, may never be known.

What is known is that though Charles Manson is behind bars for life, many of his satanistic followers still roam the streets. The satanist motorcycle groups ride on. Hollywood notables continue to dabble in the occult and "white magic."

Where does it all end?

The picture surely is not bright for those who walk without Christ.

Second Timothy 3:13 says, "Evil men and imposters will proceed from bad to worse, deceiving and being deceived."

That's a pretty black picture, except that there is a bright ray of light that puts this in its proper perspective.

Jesus said, "I am the light of the world." (John 8:12) John said of Him in John 1:5, "The light shines in the darkness," and in verse 9, "That was the true light, which coming into the world, enlightens every man."

Even in the midst of a society which seems to be growing steadily worse and worse, we can enter into that Light, walk in that Light, and have the power of that Light over any darkness.

One John 2:6-7 declares: "The one who says he abides in Him ought himself to walk in the same manner as He walked. Beloved, I am not writing a new commandment to you, but an old commandment which you have had from the beginning; the old commandment is the word which you have heard."

10

"Satan Got Me Off"

On April 4, 1971, alerted by suspicious neighbors, police found the body of sixty-nine-year-old Myron Amerman lying on the floor of his Miami Beach home with forty-nine stab wounds in his chest. The slight, never-married victim had been gagged with a pillow case and beaten about the head. A cross was found beneath his blood-smeared body.

That same day, a twenty-two-year-old brunette from San Diego, California, Kim Pharrell Brown, was arrested by the Florida Highway Patrol near Kissimmee, Florida, for driving Amerman's missing car at speeds of more than 100 miles an hour.

She was charged with Amerman's murder and did indeed admit killing him, telling authorities that "he deserved it."

In jail awaiting trial, the long-haired admitted Satanist unnerved her cellmates by sitting cross-legged on the floor and praying to Satan. She wore a devil's cult tattoo, an inverted cross with a triangle and three stars, between her thumb and forefingers of her left hand.

Kim denied that Amerman's killing was ritualistic and claimed that his slaying was the result of improper advances he made to her while she was a guest in his home for three days.

The case never went to trial.

In August of that year, Kim was allowed by the state's attorney's office to submit a plea of guilty to manslaughter and she was sentenced to seven years in jail.

Edna Buchanan, staff writer for the *Miami Herald*, interviewed Kim, and in an article which appeared in that newspaper on August 4, 1971, revealed that not only was Kim pleased with the light sentence, but she attributed it to the intercession of the devil.

"I should have got life," the article quoted Kim as saying. It also quoted her as saying, "I do have sadistic tendencies. I did enjoy it."

During the hour-long interview with the *Herald* writer, Kim revealed an extensive knowledge of witchcraft.

"I got into witchcraft and Satanism at the same time . . . and saw that it worked," Kim told Miss Buchanan. "What it is is mind power, collective mind power. Most spells are to better your position against someone you despise or want something from. I became sure it worked when I saw what happened after a coven mass, when spells were prayed."

She said a man who cheated her died in an auto accident a week after a spell was cast at a thirteen-member coven meeting.

She declared that the basis for Satanism is "self-gratification."

"Its creed," she pointed out, "is 'blessed are the strong, for they shall inherit the earth. Damned be the weak, for they shall be bled white as lambs.' "

She also declared that satanic services "are very much like the Catholic Mass, but in reverse."

Kim revealed that in her jail she had directed constant prayers to Satan before a hexagram drawn on a wall, and this had completely unnerved her cellmates.

"One chick hasn't slept since she's been here," she laughed. "I told her I can't do any sacrifices here unless I want another murder rap."

From her cell at the Florida State Penitentiary for Women, Kim corresponded with "Mama," mother of a friend in San Diego, who had taken Kim under her wing. She wrote: "As far as this trial, the time, or for that matter the crime (supposed crime) I was arrested for, I feel nothing other than resentment of being caught, and of the state's self-righteousness attitude that they have the justifiable right to punish anyone, especially me. Still have a super-ego maniac for a daughter. Ha! Ha!"

The few friends Kim Brown had in San Diego and in Hawaii found it hard to believe she was ever into witchcraft or Satanism. "Mama" contends that Kim's statements made to the Miami reporter were to get attention, and that Kim was one to "lead people on" if she did not like them.

Interviews with nearly a dozen of her acquaintances in Florida, Louisiana, Hawaii, and California, revealed much to confirm Miss Brown's post-hearing statements concerning Satanism and her capacity for murder. Even if some of her bizarre statements to the press were fabricated for attention, investigation indicated that Kim was indeed into witchcraft and Satanism.

A handwritten list of witchcraft supplies was found in Kim's wallet at the Miami Police Department. Her extraordinary interest in reading occult books, an interest in drawing satanic art illustrations, attendance at Church of Satan worship services, and the wearing of talismans were other indications of deep occult involvement.

Kim was born in San Diego on November 16, 1951, the daughter of a Marine officer of Chinese extraction and a mother of cultured French ancestry who works as a highly paid fashion model. Her father retired from the Marines, worked as a fireman, then later as a bartender, and died of cancer and cirrhosis of the liver when Kim was young.

Kim attended elementary school in San Diego and developed a reputation as a loner at an early age. As she grew older, she became sensitive about her appearance.

"She hated it when people called her 'chink.' That's what her brother called her, and she'd clobber him for it," says Mama. "That's why she always wore dark glasses, even inside the house. Her eyes are beautiful, but she won't let anybody see them because she's afraid of what they might think."

By the time she reached seventh grade at Roosevelt School, Kim was known as a quiet girl "who always had her nose in the air," according to a former classmate.

She did develop a close friendship with a girl whom we will call Ann, but even this reportedly sparked conflict with her mother.

"Kim's mother didn't want her to mingle with other

children," Mama said. "She thought she was too good for others."

Kim's problems went deeper than that. Baptized in the Episcopal Church, her mother was strict about Sunday school attendance.

"She said her mother was always talking about how important religion was, although she never went to church herself. She said she couldn't understand her mother's double standards, because both her mother and father were heavy drinkers and fought constantly, in addition to her mother being a nude model. Kim was troubled about these things and was always talking to me about it," Mama confided.

As Kim told a reporter after her sentencing, she had scorned organized religion long ago. "It's hypocrisy. My god is a material god. But I've seen Satan, at a Black Mass in San Francisco, and everybody there saw him too."

Tension, to the point of "extreme hatred," according to another observer, developed between hot-tempered Kim and her mother.

When she was fifteen, Kim started carrying a large purse with her, like most girls do. But unlike most girls, Kim carried something extra with her—a bottle of vodka—according to Mama.

"She loved to drink Smirnoff vodka and eat cheese and crackers," said Mama. "She liked to drink instead of taking dope. One day when I discovered what she was up to—she had left an empty bottle in my daughter's room—I confronted her with it, and she just got up and walked out and slammed the door. Later after her temper flare-up cooled, she came back and apologized."

When Ann's father found out about Kim's drinking, he ordered that she never be allowed again in his house.

However, attempts by the parents of the two girls to separate them were futile. Soon they were cutting high school classes and sneaking around together. Authorities finally caught up with them, and they were sent to a psychiatrist for evaluation.

Kim's only boyfriend was "skinny and ugly," according to Ann's mother. "I don't know what Kim saw in him.

The guy never went to school. He looked like a gorilla with his long hair. She called him Ringo. I think she liked the way he talked—he was very smug. They went together for about six months when she was sixteen. They broke up when he had to go back to Samoa. He said he had accumulated too many traffic tickets here."

Kim and Ann would double date occasionally, but "you couldn't separate them. They were inseparable," Mama said.

To help keep the two apart, Mama signed Ann up for singing lessons. "She had a very good voice and great potential. In fact, her professor thought so much of her that he went to Hollywood and hired a band for her so she could record an album. He had designed a picture for the album and set up everything. She was going to sing twenty songs.

"The day came to make the recording. Kim and Ann went off. I got a call later on—they had never arrived in Hollywood. Instead, they went to Catalina Island. The professor was very angry," she recalled.

Although Kim was considered a very smart girl by her friends, she and Ann quit school at the age of sixteen. They both continued to get into trouble by shoplifting. Finally probation authorities threatened to take Ann away from her family and put her into a girls' home.

To remedy the situation, Ann's mother took her to Hawaii to stay with relatives.

Kim ended up in juvenile hall as a runaway.

"Going to juvenile hall made her happy," a friend recalls. "She wanted to see how her mother would react. I think it was her way of getting back at her mother. She really despised her mother and father, and she hated all men. She hates children too."

Kim's first and only love, say her acquaintances, was reading.

"She's a loner. She was always reading long and hard books like *Rise and Fall of the Third Reich*, *The Source*, all of Harold Robbins books such as *The Adventurers*, and she thought Edgar Allen Poe's stuff was the greatest. She could recite Poe's 'The Raven' by heart," says a friend.

A wide variety of occult books were also a part of her reading habits, for she was extremely fascinated with supernatural things.

Before Ann departed for Hawaii, she and Kim went to San Francisco, according to Mama. "Kim had read up on witchcraft and Satanism, so when they were in San Francisco, the girls went to look in on the Church of Satan. They said they were scared at first because of the way everyone was dressed. Kim said that the ceremony resembled the Catholic Church's."

As Kim told a reporter after her court appearance, "I was scared to death when I first got into it. The ceremonies, which I can't talk about, shocked me. But now it's catching on. Covens are springing up all over the country, particularly around universities. What you call the peace symbol is also a Satanist symbol—a cross with broken arms."

When it came time for Ann to leave for Hawaii, Kim slashed her wrists, according to Mama. However, she recovered, and counted the days until she turned eighteen and could leave home for good. Since her father's death she had more or less lived at home with her mother, collecting $100 a month from her father's estate. She saved the checks and bought a ticket to Hawaii, which she used the day she turned eighteen.

Kim thoroughly enjoyed Hawaii. She spent long days sunning on the beach reading books and at night played cards with Ann or went down to the Diamond Cue pool hall in Honolulu where she earned the nickname "Cat Girl" because of her quiet manner.

"Kim was a wonderful pool shooter," another friend recalls. "One night, she beat twelve men in a row. One guy was so upset that he went to another pool hall and practiced for an hour, then came back and bet her $100 that he could beat her. Kim beat him!"

The two girls were offered jobs as models with high pay, but when they found out the job involved pornography they turned down the offer.

Kim also had an offer to become a $500 a night call girl for a gambling syndicate operating between Las Vegas and Honolulu. Although she rejected this offer, the man who made the proposition let her use his plush apartment in Honolulu.

To earn some money and "just for kicks," Kim and her friend took jobs as maids in a Honolulu hotel. There, police theorize, Kim turned "cat burglar," a term used to describe burglars who enter a person's room at night to steal.

Using their master keys, they had easy access to rooms which they knew contained valuables. For starters, police say, Kim stole credit cards.

It was during this time that Ann became pregnant and decided to marry the young marine she said was the baby's father.

"It was a crushing blow to Kim when Ann got married," says Mama. "She tried to stop the marriage by telling Ann to leave the baby with her, and she would take care of it. But slowly she accepted the fact of the marriage. Then one day she decided to go to New Orleans. That was the last we saw of her."

According to police in New Orleans, she arrived there with stolen credit cards and got herself a job as a maid at one of the major hotels. She located a bar there and made friends with the local crowd, while living out of a nearby hotel.

One night while up to her old tricks as a cat burglar she got caught leaving an upper story room. According to police, she had tied several sheets together and fastened them to the balcony. After taking the loot she planned to slip down the sheet-rope and swing away, Tarzan style. Her plans went astray; she fell four stories onto soft ground, suffering sprained ankles. The police were waiting for her and promptly booked her into jail.

In late March, Kim flew to Miami for reasons unknown. Some of the police theorized that she was planning to fly to nearby Haiti to witness voodoo ceremonies.

In Miami Beach she made contact with Amerman. One theory goes that she had his name and was told to look him up, but where she got it or when is unknown. Others believe that Amerman may have befriended her and offered her free room and board if she would stay at his apartment and help clean up. A third theory goes that Kim may have been trying to get rid of some stolen jewelry and wanted to use the wealthy Amerman as her fence.

Kim and Amerman were seen together in Miami Beach, but nothing distinctive about the scene is remembered by witnesses.

Events of the night of April 6 still are not clear to officers who investigated the case. Miss Brown told several different stories, including the one that Amerman made advances and they fought.

Whatever the reason, Kim told the Miami reporter that she experienced sexual satisfaction while stabbing Amerman in the chest with a ten-inch steak knife and that "I laughed . . . I did enjoy it."

Asked if Amerman was already dead when she burst into laughter, Kim said, "He saw me. That was the whole point. I wouldn't have laughed if he'd been dead. Mental sadism is a lot more fun. It was his own fault."

Amerman's death, she said, was "catch back," revenge for an incident that took place between them several years ago. "I had something against the man. He paid me back with his life."

After killing Amerman, Kim spent two hours in the house with the body, then she took a shower, dressed, and departed. Most of the forty-six stab wounds were in groupings around the chest and neck.

Police authorities spent more than three months investigating the case and trying to put together evidence to convict her on first-degree murder charges. A public uproar resulted when the state's attorney accepted the manslaughter plea.

Throughout the investigation, police were struck by Kim's lack of emotion at being arrested on the murder charge.

"I thought I'd ride along and see what happened," she said.

"I'm here for one purpose," she told the *Miami Herald* reporter, "to enjoy myself. I can't remember when I've ever cried. I like me. This is only an experience in my life—which has a long way to go."

Although Kim claims she never cried, she later wrote this letter to Mama in California:

My mother was down here for the trial—it's the first time I've seen her all year, and I might add the first time I've been able to talk with and see her without an argument—HEADLINES—huge accomplishments—WE SHALL OVERCOME YET (smile). For once in my life I felt kinda rotten—for one reason—she cried, and for her, well that's about as bad as me crying—it takes a lot. About the only time I can remember is that time at Doug's where you hit me. It was the pain inside, not outside.

Later in the letter, she describes how a national publication, *Detective Magazine*, wrote up her case using phony pictures posed by a model.

The story that is told isn't necessarily the truth (except the facts) but it is many peoples' evaluation of what they think happened. I will say this now—I am the only living person that actually knows what happened. One day, I will rap it down to you but until then you might get a kick out of reading the story.

Do you ever remember me saying, someday people will know about me? This is not what I meant—not at all. . . .

Kim's friends to this day refuse to believe that she was a Satan worshiper, although one woman close to her admitted: "She likes to act out what she has read. She got the idea of tying the sheets together in New Orleans out of an old Tarzan book."

A list of items found in Miss Brown's wallet included various supplies and clothing needed by any traveler, as well as the *Satanic Bible*, a satanic cross, a Pisces ring, and black candles from Witches Workshop. The final notation on the page reads, "Witches Workshop, 500 block of St. Phillip." (Witches Workshop is a store in New Orleans which specializes in selling occult and witchcraft supplies.)

Asked in a telephone interview if she were practicing Satanism in prison, Kim Brown answered, "If I do, it's none of your concern. If I do, it's up to me and what I'm doing. It's nobody's business but mine. I will not tell you anything about anything."

Before she left for prison, Miss Brown was asked for proof that devil worship works.

She responded: "I've lived good all my life and never worked. I got out of about fifteen charges in Louisiana, from burglary to fraudulent use of a credit card. I went to court July 26—first day of our highest holidays, Lammas, which is July 26 to August 1. It was a good sign."

Then, asked by reporter Edna Buchanan why Satan hadn't delivered her from her current predicament, Kim Brown smiled and said, "He *has* to a point, hasn't he?"

This young girl's life was marred with truancy, pool hustling, shoplifting, temper flare-ups, burglaries, Satan worship, witchcraft practices, and murder, and with possible indications of homosexuality and prostitution.

Kim's life started in an all-American surrounding, and she ultimately ended up in prison for murder.

What lies ahead for Kim Brown?

Only God knows.

It is impossible to bring this chapter to a definite close, because, at this writing, Kim Brown is at large, having escaped from the penitentiary in Florida shortly after material for this chapter was researched.

In fact, because our files on her background and friends are so comprehensive, a detective from the San Diego sheriff's department spent several hours pouring over our material for leads in trying to find her.

Considering the violence and lawlessness of her background, it is almost inconceivable that the record won't be continued with other crimes. The headlines may yet again bring out a bloody story of satanic worship and senseless killing, *unless*!

Unless, somehow, somewhere . . . satanic murderess Kim Brown comes into contact with the saving grace of the Lord Jesus Christ and takes the way out of the satanic web in which she is entangled!

Hopefully, prayerfully, she will be one who has tasted deeply of the things of evil but will find the road to peace and love.

The picture is grim, but not hopeless. I will be relating to you later cases I know in which God has wrought marvelous deliverance to such captives.

He is able!

One John 3:8 says, "The Son of God appeared for this purpose, that He might destroy the works of the devil."

90

11

The Inhumane Society

Humans are not the only beings to meet with gory violence at the hands of occultists!

Practitioners have left behind a long and bloody trail of tortured and misused animals that sickens the imagination. Some of these instances have already been mentioned, but these are just a drop in the bucket compared to a long list of such brutalities that have been reported.

The brutal slaughter of animals including birds, goats, hamsters, rabbits, dogs, and cats during satanic rites proves that among the sick minds of practicing occultists there is no humane society.

The *Satanic Bible* by Anton LaVey states that "an animal is never slaughtered for the purpose of using all or a part of that animal in their satanic ritual." However, many police investigators have noticed an increase in unusual animal deaths and place the blame on witchcraft and other satanic practices.

Voodoo rites in Haiti and in the American Southeast and Southwest often included the slaughter of chickens, with the blood supposedly being drunk by the high priest or sprinkled about during the ceremony.

In the southern California seaside community of Venice,

police have reported finding the bodies of slain animals along the beaches.

In October of 1971, officers went to the beach after a woman called to say she saw a van of hippie types unload a box which appeared to be dripping blood.

When officers dug up the "casket," they found not a human body, but that of a large German shepherd dog which had apparently been sacrificed in a satanic rite. These details were described by Captain Bob Vernon.

"Its throat had been cut and there was some evidence of skinning the dog," Vernon says. "According to several guys I talked to who were at ceremonies like these up in the hills, they try to pull the hide off the dog before it dies. They try to keep it alive and let it walk around without its skin on. The groups are definitely tied in with witchcraft and Satanism.

"When you talk to these people, they readily admit that they are followers of the occult," Vernon said, "and, that they have various types of ceremonies, even to the point of mixing the animal blood with LSD and drinking it in order to heighten their trances."

A Florida farmer told an interviewer that black chickens, white guineas, and some types of young goats and lambs are practically unobtainable on the market because so many are being used in rituals.

Latin cults in Miami have paid as much as $150 a night to use remote sheds or shacks in the agricultural sections of the county for their sacrificial rites. One researcher discovered that as much as $3,000 has been paid to a "priest" to perform certain occult rites.

A writer in Miami who raises homing pigeons, as a sideline has been making a small fortune selling the same birds over and over to Cuban occultists. The homing pigeons are used in a ritual where they are passed over the person's body—assuming all the person's ills and bad luck—and released to fly speedily away.

Other less expensive birds and animals are sacrificed—chickens or goats—with the blood caught in small bowls.

The entrails of the sacrificed animals are used in various voodoo-type ceremonies by superstitious Cubans, then cooked and eaten along with the bodies.

In satanic worship services held in San Bernardino, California, animals were sacrificed "as a proxy for a human," according to one practitioner. "Instead of sacrificing an infant, which is suggested in ancient rituals, the sacrifice is made the same way but with an animal. You can't get thrown in jail for killing an animal—yet," the former Satanist said.

"A lot of times, the blood of the animal, after being consecrated to the devil, is used in the communion ceremony," the ex-Satanist claimed. "Flesh is eaten raw on the communion wafers.

"Animals used in the sacrifices are never handled very humanely. They're not drugged first—they're just hauled up on the altar, and the cruelty begins as they are cut, poked, and ripped apart. They are killed in a very crude manner. Disemboweling is not an instantaneous death.

"The ceremony calls for going through the satanic ritual, consecration, sex, and then a dog is slit open. The high priest takes out certain sections or organs and uses them in sacrifice.

"Then the blood is drained at the same time. The animal usually doesn't die until some of the organs are cut out, so the animal is alive during the first part of the procedure, " the former Satanist recalled. "It's agony for the animal."

Occult movies often depict animal sacrifices. One person interviewed described a sacrifice involving a cat which took place on a private beach on the boundary line of Los Angeles and Ventura counties on Highway 1. The group met when the moon was full.

"It was gruesome," he declared. "They took lighted firecrackers and sat a living cat on them. The cat was blown to smithereens. It was sickening."

If the *Satanic Bible* prohibits animal sacrifices, why is it done by Satanists?

To begin with, most occultists do not adhere to Anton LaVay's *Satanic Bible*. Actually very few of those who are officially connected with his organized Church of Satan prescribe to his bible's doctrine on animal sacrifices. Many have been known to participate in their own variety of satanic sacrificial rites.

Several other occult practices such as witchcraft and voodoo do not adhere to this bible and do use animal sacrifices.

We mentioned that one of the motivating factors that attracts people into the occult is *the desire for power and control over others*. Since the practitioner of witchcraft may wish to avoid prosecution for murder as the result of sacrificing a human being, he seeks a substitute. What better substitute than a helpless animal?

The act of killing the animal symbolizes power to the sick mind of the perpetrator. The person doing the killing may have deep-rooted resentments against other people, and killing the animal may symbolize to him killing the hated person.

The requirement of having their subjects drink animal blood, as has been discovered in some instances, serves as a "test" to separate the "men from the boys." Those who want to get into witchcraft and Satanism badly enough must endure the most disgusting practices as a test of their sincerity. Those who can make it through the trials and initiation rites, no matter how sick they may be, are finally "acceptable."

It is difficult to determine to what extent animal sacrifices are used in occult practices because these practices vary so much from place to place and from country to country.

There is no doubt that the practitioners of blood sacrifices do murder humans at times, as apparently was the case in the California schoolteacher and Montana social worker as noted previously.

In the San Jose area, police discovered two female bodies which had been stabbed a total of 300 times and partially drained of their blood. It was believed that these women were prostitutes or "non-established" types, ideal victims for Satanists because no one would miss them.

There is no doubt that the minds which concoct these senseless and barbaric tortures of animals and humans are sick, twisted by the forces of evil which control them.

It is hard to believe that someone entering the occult world would, as one of their first acts, engage in such practices. But the fact remains that a person is initiated into the occult by committing a definite act, no matter how insignificant it appears. This innocent beginning has the strong possibility of leading the "dabbler" down the dark labyrinth to this evil sickness.

12

The Sex Trap

Like everything else he can get his sordid hands on, Satan has defiled, defamed, and twisted what God meant to be the good and right and natural way of reproduction here on earth.

The Bible clearly states that the body is the temple of God and that it should not be defiled under penalty of God's wrath. This is recorded in 1 Corinthians 3:16-17, which says, "Do you not know that you are a temple of God, and that the Spirit of God dwells in you? If any man destroys the temple of God, God will destroy him; for the temple of God is holy, and that is what you are."

Sex, as God intended it, is neither ugly nor impure. Someone has wisely said that sex is God's wedding present to man and wife. Any other use of it is stolen.

This tremendous life force lies within each creature, but when its potential is yielded into the hands of Satan it becomes a weapon for him to use in his headlong course of destruction and sorrow.

Nowhere is the sex urge more prominent than in young people on the threshold of adulthood. Many are intrigued, and many are frightened, when they begin to notice the natural changes taking place in their strong young bodies.

At no time in life is there more apt to be experimentation with sex.

Satan knows this, and he preys on it. That's one reason why so many young people find themselves in trouble, because of misused sex, with problem pregnancies, perversions, and other unfortunate occurrences.

We know for a fact that Satanists dwell on sex and deliberately use it as a snare to hook young people into their growing ranks!

The sad part is that what starts out as pleasure often turns into a serpent whose bite leaves bitter, poisonous ruin in the lives and minds and hearts of our youth!

I'm going to quote here at length from the documented statement of a young man who was recruiter for one of the largest satanic organizations in Southern California.

Here is how his recruiting strategy worked, as told in his own words: "One of the primary means of getting people into witchcraft and Satanism is through offering free sex.

"We would select our members very carefully. I was a student in junior college at the time and very much into witchcraft. My job was to recruit new members so that ultimately we could get them trapped into dealing drugs and practicing hard core witchcraft and Satanism.

"I would look around the classroom for a guy of average intelligence. It's good to use this strategy in psychology or sociology classes because people there are usually interested in themselves or have problems relating to others. You might say they're 'searching for truth.'

"For a potential member, I preferred to work on someone who was rather quiet because he usually had a lot of things on his mind that he was trying to figure out. The loud ones were apt to shoot off their mouths, anyway.

"After I zeroed in on my carefully selected target, I'd make up some kind of excuse to get friendly. If the guy asked a question in class, I'd make careful note of it and then try to analyze what was really bugging him. If he picked a particular topic for a term paper, I'd find out what it was, go to the library and read upon the subject. It was easy to talk with someone like that, because to all appearances you had a mutual interest.

"I'd say something to make the person bring up the topic of sex, usually pointing to the attributes of some attractive chick who was walking or sitting nearby.

"If the guy was interested in girls, he would have several reactions. This was another key to his personality.

"If he expressed any interest in sex, then the conversation warmed up fast. I would drop in a few things about current sex books to see how serious the guy was.

"On my third or fourth conversation with him, after I'd established a casual but personal rapport, I finally would bring up the topic of sex activities to get into conversation on sex again. Then I would confide that I knew a place where we could go for free to observe or participate in an orgy.

" 'Sure,' he would say. 'Let's go. When? Where?'

"I would tell him that we had to go to this guy's apartment first to get the address. I'd tell him in detail about the fancy layout, the free food and booze, and how the guy kept a nymphomaniac around.

"It worked most of the time because we played on basic human emotions and needs: the desire for sex, food, money, and attention. Find out what the guy's needs are, and then tell him you've got an easy way to fulfill them!

"If a guy was reluctant to go to the apartment or had any reservations at all, I would use the old 'don't be chicken' line and maybe even question his masculinity. No guy wants to admit to another that he isn't anything but all male.

"Once we got to the apartment, we would have a few drinks from the well-stocked bar, and of course Gloria would always be there. We would play the stereo, rap, and relax. All the time, Gloria was looking at the new guy and directing the conversation at him. I've never seen anybody resist her advances.

"Then it was up to Gloria and the guy. You just used a little applied psychology and pretty soon you had the guy hooked.

"I would let him see Gloria a couple more times—but only if he went with me. On the third visit, Gloria would come on with her story about how she's a witch, and was just getting ready to cast a spell.

"Of course we would act interested. If the other guy

showed any reluctance, I would volunteer to be 'it.' Whatever the spell was about, Gloria would turn out all the lights, light a couple of black candles, then go into her chants.

"She would be wearing a black robe when we came to the apartment, and eventually, she would shed it.

"When finally I would have the guy involved and in my confidence, then I would go all the way and invite him to a self-styled coven meeting.

"All I would tell him was that there was going to be this party on Friday night and why didn't we double date. He should bring Gloria and I would bring another chick. I would pick him up in my car so he couldn't get away.

"After we picked up Gloria, we would drive to a house in a secluded area. You needed seclusion and confusion in getting to the place, so that the person could never find his way back there by himself.

"That would be the night we had the orgy. Everybody got into it. After that, I would drop on him the whole scene about the regular Friday night parties, sex, and how he could make good money on the side through the contacts he had in the coven. By now the guy would be a pushover. Finally, we would initiate him into the group.

"We got all kinds of people involved, including professional workers and civic leaders, because we were so secretive and discreet in the way we recruited members. We gave the person a feeling of power.

"The person in witchcraft feels he has power to control others, and can perform all kinds of rituals to get anything he wants—sex, money, you name it.

"You think it's great, until you fall, or get caught pushing drugs, stealing car stereos, or whatever—and by the time you are really into it deep, you're involved in every vice or perversion you can think of.

"In witchcraft you are used just to satisfy someone else's desires, and that covers everything. The only way out for many has been self-inflicted death."

The young man who related this is now a born-again Christian filled with the Holy Spirit, whose desire is to keep people out of the same kind of bondage he once wanted to lead them into.

Thank God for those who have found a way out!

Another of these was a young lady, now a waitress in San Bernardino, who had a horrifying experience with a witchcraft coven.

This young girl was known in high school as being sexually promiscuous. One night she was walking down the street when two members of a witchcraft order pulled up besider her, swept her right off the street into their car and drove her to a large warehouse where satanic rites were being conducted.

"Our sacrifice has arrived!" one of the men inside announced.

The leader ordered the girl to strip or have her clothes ripped to shreds. Terrified, she fell to her knees and pleaded for mercy. Instead, leaders ordered both of her hands to be broken to make her less resistant to their efforts, and then the girl was used as an "altar" for the satanic rites and raped repeatedly by thirteen men!

Despite this abasement and the terrible shame which followed, this girl later became a Christian and found healing and mental health in Jesus.

After her conversion, she saw one of her tormentors on the street and walked up and told him she forgave him because she now belonged to Jesus. The man turned and fled. Later he reported that her remarks about Jesus "blew my mind, man!" He also found Jesus as his Savior; who knows what part the girl's testimony played in his conversion even though it took place many months later!

Another girl who found herself shamefully debased was the product of a broken home. She had become tired of babysitting for a younger brother and sister while her mother worked.

One day, at the urging of a friend, the two of them crashed a party at a boy's home; the girl took up with a sixteen-year-old youth whose ability to use four-letter words impressed her, and she ended up in the back seat of a car with the situation out of control.

Three months later when she found out she was pregnant, she was talked into running away by the boy involved. He drove her to a rundown house outside Cocoa Beach, Florida, occupied by four hippie boys.

What happened to Arlene is too ugly to describe in

detail. After a "marriage" ceremony conducted in the name of Satan, she was forced to submit to sex with the entire group. The violent treatment she received that night at the hands of the five young men caused a miscarriage.

The girl eventually returned to her mother out of sheer desperation.

"We were into all kinds of satanic worship services when I was living with Bill and his friends," this girl said. "I always ended up on the altar, though. I couldn't take it any more."

Upon her return home, she developed an intense hatred for her mother.

"She'd be out drinking and living it up with guys while I was still home babysitting for the kids," she said.

One day the girl thought back to some of the satanic ritual to which she had been exposed while with Bill. She could see him, dressed in a black robe, holding a knife up high, ready to plunge it into a black cat which lay purring on the "altar."

Driven by wild emotion, she picked up a kitchen knife and approached her mother, who was peeling carrots.

As her mother worked, the girl brought her arm back and prepared to plunge the knife into her mother's back.

Just as she brought the knife down, her mother stepped to the side to pick up a bowl, and the knife missed her.

"What are you trying to do?" the mother shouted at her.

"Then I went mad," the girl said. "I still had the knife in my hand, and I took off after my mother. I don't know what came over me—it was just an awful hate. I had to kill her. I chased her all over the house with the knife. Finally, she locked herself in a bedroom and called her brother, who came over and talked to me.

"When I realized what I had done, I broke down and cried," she said. "I don't know what made me do it."

Terrifying experiences—but, thank God, there was also a way out for her!

Another testimony of the horrors of sex in Satanism was given by a young man we shall call Brian.

Now nineteen, Brian had dropped out of high school when he was fifteen. With an IQ of between 160-168, he

102

Burdened with the spiritual needs of Israel, Morris Cerrullo stands in an Israeli wheatfield holding up grain ripe for the harvest.

Almost obscured by smoke, Morris Cerrullo witnesses the burning of occult items in Haiti during the meeting described in Chapter 1.

In Pusan, Korea, 1971, ministers sit on the floor from wall to wall. The ministers' training meetings were so popular that some of the men actually broke windows and doors to get in after the hall was filled.

In 1965, Morris Cerrullo presents a Deeper Life Edition of the Bible to the late President Eisenhower.

Morris Cerrullo conducts an indoor meeting, a "School of Evangelism" in Monado, Indonesia, 1972.

A crusade outdoors, with crowds of standing people, held in Monado, Indonesia, in 1972.

A sea of people in Seoul, Korea, 1971, raise hands in praise to God at outdoor meeting.

During meetings in Great Britian in 1969, Morris Cerrullo discusses the Bible with Prime Minister Harold Wilson.

Morris Cerrullo wears a tribal robe just presented to him in Kumasi, Ghana, in 1967.

The witchmobile travels across the country demonstrating occult items.

Inside the witchmobile are displays of books and other parphenelia used in witchcraft (see next page).

found school "a complete bore." He left home to stay with relatives in Syracuse, New York.

To support himself, he went to work as a "printer's devil," an apprentice in a print shop there. At the same time he decided to study graphic arts at Syracuse University. There he began his entrance into the occult.

"One of the guys in the shop was interested in extrasensory perception, mental telepathy, and telekenisis," he related. "He invited me to a gathering one night where some of the people were getting together to discuss ESP and everything. I was very easily sucked into this, being new in town and not really having any friends. And it really sounded interesting.

"We were sitting around talking about these things that night and somebody started bringing out words like 'sorcery' and 'witchcraft.' I thought *Ha, ha, ha, this is funny. These things are all myths. They don't exist.* Then I started finding out these people were members of a coven. After about three weeks, they told me that after I left every Friday night, they had begun coven meetings of their own. I'd been looked over and was considered acceptable by the group, if I wanted to stay.

"I was a new Christian at the time but really very immature, and was not witnessing at that time. I thought, *Gee whiz, it's irrelevant here.* They had already shown me how foolish it was to hold to all those traditional beliefs, which, according to them, were obviously not valid. I bought it hook, line, and sinker.

"I stayed that night, and it was the first time I had ever been to a Black Mass. I was given an invitation to join the coven and I did. There was only one thing in the invitation which slightly bothered me, and it was that I was supposed to reject Christ, reject Jesus, and deny His power.

"I said, 'What does it matter? What's going to happen to me anyway? I've already been shown that it's a bunch of malarkey.' I was slowly indoctrinated into the group, and during the time I was in Syracuse, they started teaching me the black arts. I was brought up to a warlock second level.

"The furthest I ever got into the occult was nerve

paralysis, the actual taking over of somebody's nervous system. It was a very real thing.

"When I came back down to Florida, I got into a coven which practiced so-called 'white magic.' I didn't tell them my background had been in black magic. I decided to go from black magic into white magic, only to realize that after doing my good deeds in praying to angels and all the other things, there was never a contact with God, even in white magic.

"White magic, I'm now convinced, is more deceiving than black magic because in white magic there is the appearance of good. But its selfishness, self-glorification, and idolatry make it the more devious of the two forms.

"In black magic, at least they're openly worshiping Satan, while white magic is actually beguiling. I was easily sucked in."

Describing one of the Friday night black magic coven meetings in Syracuse, the youth said the ceremony was held in a twenty by forty foot basement of a home.

"Two of the walls were done in red and gold while the other two walls were in red and black. There were twelve ultraviolet black lights fastened to the ceiling. Everything in the room was black light sensitive. There was a greenish glow on the altar. The room was very eerie.

"We would dress in black robes. Then the leader would bring in a seventeen- or eighteen-year-old girl who would stand in the middle of the room. Then the chant would start. It centered on the destruction of purity; anything that's good is worth destroying. That was the underlying purpose of the group.

"Then everyone would go around her and tear something from her. She would be stripped from the neck down. Each time you passed, you screamed profanity at her and things like 'we're going to destroy you!' as you tore something off. Then she was left there nude."

The youth related that then unspeakable indignities to the girl followed.

"Afterward, the priest would come back and hold a live chicken by the feet over her," he continued. "Then he would wring the head off. The chicken, which was still alive, would flap and beat its wings, making the blood spew out from the head. He would sprinkle the dripping blood on everyone, especially the girl. The focal point was the girl. The blood being splattered on her represented her death.

"It's illegal to kill people as a sacrifice so they use a chicken. The choice of a chicken is unimportant except for the chicken claw, which has been called the 'witch's claw' or peace symbol.

"Then the chicken claw would be raked over the girl to put scratches on her stomach. This girl's stomach was pretty well scarred because she had gone through this lots of times. That ended the ceremony.

"It took about four hours. There were from fifteen to twenty persons involved—a banker, a doctor, a lawyer, a photographer, two teachers, and assorted other types."

Brian is grateful to God for another opportunity to serve Him. Having rededicated his life to Christ and having found forgiveness, he is now working at a home for handicapped children in Miami.

While most of the current books on witchcraft deny there is any sex involved in the ceremonies, the young people interviewed for this chapter said that group sex practices are common.

"The candles, the ritual, the chants, the whole atmosphere heighten your desire for sex. It makes witchcraft more fun," said one girl.

It is obvious that by preying on man's weaknesses and desires, witchcraft can easily attract anyone who is seeking sex kicks, power, and fulfillment of lust.

It is not only in witchcraft that young people are being drawn into acts which dishonor their bodies, but in many worldly circles it has become the accepted norm.

Drive-in movies have been termed "motels on wheels" because young people sometimes commit immoral acts in parked automobiles. Even such public places as beaches and parks have openly become petting grounds, often to the extent that families have been driven from recreation centers in search of more fitting sights for the eyes of growing youngsters.

The need for chastity has not diminished, despite the age of permissiveness now upon us.

113

Someone asked me recently for a quotation about the urgency for young people to retain their purity in the midst of a world seemingly gone sexually unrestrained.

I pointed them to the Bible and noted two passages taken from the *Living Letters* edition.

One passage is 1 Thessalonians 4:3-5, which says, "For God wants you to be holy and pure, and to keep clear of all sexual sin so that each of you will marry in holiness and honor—not in lustful passion as the heathen do, in their ignorance of God and His ways."

The other was Colossians 3:5, which says, "Away then with sinful, earthly things; deaden the evil desires lurking within you; have nothing to do with sexual sin, impurity, lust and shameful desires; don't worship the good things of this life, for that is idolatry."

What quotation could be found from a better source than God's Word?

13

First Church of Satan

The world was shocked on the last night of April, 1966, when a San Franciscan by the name of Anton Szandor LaVey shaved his head, put on a clerical collar, and announced the formation of the "First Church of Satan."

The night chosen for the proclamation was "Walpurgisnacht," said to be the most important festival in the lore of magic and witchcraft. Occultists claim that this is the time demons and evil spirits celebrate the fruition of the spring equinox.

Since that night, LaVey has become known as the Black Pope, has published his own *Satanic Bible*, and has made sensational news over his worship services with nude women on the altar.

Though some occultists draw a line between so-called "white magic" which they say is good, and "black magic" which they admit is bad, LaVey makes no such distinction.

"There is no difference between white and black magic," LaVey has said, "except in the smug hypocrisy, guilt-ridden righteousness, and self-deceit of the white magician himself. White magic is supposedly practiced for good, altruistic, benevolent purposes while black magic is done for destruction and evil purposes. No one on earth ever pursued occult studies, metaphysics, yoga—or any other white light concept—without ego gratification and personal power as a goal."

Thus LaVey frankly admitted his goals in organizing the infamous Church of Satan which he now claims has 10,000 dues-paying members in the United States and a worldwide following of 100,000 to 200,000.

Located in a black, three-story Victorian house in San Francisco, the church engages in Black Mass, and has captured the attention of many non-Christians, including dozens of show business personalities.

LaVey said that the purpose of the Church of Satan was to get together "a group of like-minded individuals for the use of their combined energies in calling up the dark force in nature that is called Satan."

LaVey, now forty-one years old, got the idea that the devil is alive and popular with people twenty years ago while he was playing organ for carnival sideshows. He began formulating his own religion which serves as the antithesis to Christianity and its Judaic heritage. LaVey proclaims his basic theme: "There is a demon inside men which must be exercised—not exorcised—and channeled into ritualized hatred."

Descended of Georgian, Rumanian, and Alsatian grandparents, LaVey was raised on ancient legends of vampires and witches in his native Transylvania. At the age of five, according to the *Satanic Bible*, LaVey was already reading such things as *Weird Tales* magazines, *Frankenstein*, and *Dracula*.

"He felt different from other children, and yet he became a ringleader, glorying in the organization of mock military orders," says the *Satanic Bible*.

When he was twelve, LaVey became interested in toy soldiers and war. After reading military manuals, he became fascinated by the idea that masses of people could be conquered with easily accessible military equipment. He decided that contrary to what the Bible teaches, the earth would be inherited *not by the meek, but by the strong and mighty*.

Entering high school near San Francisco, LaVey carried

on his interests outside the classroom with the secrets of the occult, metaphysics, and music.

He became a high school dropout at sixteen, left home, and joined the Clyde Beatty Circus as a cage boy, watering and feeding the lions and tigers. Later he became an assistant trainer and also played the calliope.

At eighteen, LaVey left the circus and joined a carnival where he became assistant to a magician, learned hypnosis, and studied more about the occult.

After marrying his first wife, he quit the carnival and enrolled as a criminology major at San Francisco City College. That led to his first "conformist" job as a photographer for the San Francisco Police Department.

"As it worked out, that job had as much to do as any other with leading me toward Satanism," his *Satanic Bible* says.

"I saw the bloodiest, grimiest side of human nature," He recalled. "People shot by nuts, knifed by friends, little kids splattered in the gutter by hit-and-run drivers. It was disgusting and depressing."

He quit the police department after three years and turned to playing the organ in nightclubs, meanwhile continuing his studies in the black arts. He held classes in ritual magic once a week in his home. One of those attracted by these classes was John Raymond, free-lance writer and publicist who now lives in Berkeley and helps Philip Emmons Isaac Bonewits, the "Wizard of Berkeley," with his promotions.

With Raymond's help, LaVey made front-page news and created a public stir when Raymond and his bride were married in the Church of Satan. The bride was Judith Case, daughter of a prominent lawyer and political figure, Edward H. Case of New York.

Eventually, a "Magic Circle" evolved from a small group of LaVey's elite followers.

According to the *Satanic Bible*, the major purpose of the circle was to meet for the performance of black rituals that LaVey had discovered. He had accumulated a library of works that described the Black Mass and other pagan ceremonies conducted by groups such as the Knights Templar in 14th Century France and the Golden Dawn in 19th Century England.

The original intent of these pagan rituals was to mock and blaspheme the Christian church. The "worshipers" addressed themselves to Satan as an anthropomorphic deity who represented the reverse of God. In LaVey's view, Satan was much more than the reverse of God. He represented a dark, hidden force in nature responsible for the workings of earthly affairs for which science and religion had no explanation and no control.

By LaVey's own admission, "There is no altruism or love-thy-neighbor concept in the satanic religion, except in the sense of helping other adherents of the Black Path to gain their desires by group energy."

"Satanism is a blatantly selfish, brutal religion," the *Satanic Bible* states. "It is based on the belief that man is inherently a selfish, violent creature, that life is a Darwinian struggle for survival of the fittest, that the earth will be ruled by those who fight to win the ceaseless competition that exists in all jungles—including that of urban societies."

The key word in LaVey's fellowship is "indulgence." According to the *Satanic Bible*, "The seven deadly sins of the Christian church are: greed, pride, envy, anger, gluttony, lust, and sloth. Satanism advocates indulging in each of these 'sins' as they lead to physical, mental, or emotional gratification."

The Church of Satan caters to the desires of the wide variety of individuals who have taken it up—doctors, lawyers, engineers, teachers, writers, actors, stockbrokers, clerks, printers, nurses, and many other categories.

LaVey has conducted marriages, baptisms, and funerals, all in the line of duty as the high priest.

Entry into the church, either physically or by membership, is not easy. A high chain-link fence topped with barbed wire in front of the church "headquarters" makes it nearly impossible for anyone to enter except by an appointment and through an electronically activated gates.

The city of San Francisco ordered LaVey to take down the barbed wire because it was "a public nuisance and considered dangerous."

LaVey's house-church has a living room that boasts black walls and a red ceiling. The coffee table in front of the black sofa is a tombstone on legs. Other features include a swinging bookcase and numerous hidden passage-ways.

Those curious about membership may call the church, which is listed in the white pages of the telephone book. Sometimes LaVey's secretary will answer. Other times a recorded message asks the caller to leave his message. Requests for membership information and a fifty-question application are promptly mailed out to those who inquire.

The membership "prospectus" is addressed to "Seeker of Truth." The letter suggests that the prospective member read the *Satanic Bible*, which can be purchased for $1.50 from the "church." It sells for 95 cents from normal book outlets.

With disarming piety, the mimeographed letter also states: "Thus the sincerity of purpose, the intelligence of execution of all facets of the satanic philosophy become known and understood by every discerning reader (of the *Satanic Bible*). The Church of Satan is a legally recognized institution which challenges all social and religious hypocrisy; men and women of vision, sanity, and logic have swollen its ranks to many thousands, the world over. You have nothing to lose but your guilt, anxieties, and fears if you dare to forge your own destiny with us."

Membership entitles the member to information regarding church representation or grotto in his own area where the member can meet other Satanists, enter into ritual and ceremonial activities, develop knowledge of satanic magic, and progress deeper into the workings of the Church of Satan. Regularly printed bulletins and newsletters are distributed by various grottos and agencies of the church, which are made available only to qualified members.

Minors are welcome to apply for membership, provided they send written evidence of parental consent when applying for active membership.

The letter urges the recipient to read *The Complete Witch: or What to do When Virtue Fails* by LaVey and *The Second Coming: Satanism in America* by Arthur Lyons. United Press International and many religious publications reviewed the book by Lyons, but some reviews seemed to miss the point that the book appeared to be an endorsement of the Church of Satan, not only a description.

Some of the fifty questions on the questionnaire include: "Have you gone out of your way to study occultism? If so, which aspect(s) interest you most? Do you own books on occult subjects? Do you like horror films? Are you willing to submit to anything within reason if in so doing it will bring you more success in life? Do you believe in the power or force that is termed 'magic'? Do you think you are highly sexed? If you are a woman, would you consider serving as an altar for a ceremony? Do you feel that there are people or forces working against you? Is there anything you fear as a consequence of your involvement in Satanism?"

On the back page of the application is the admonition "PLEASE DON'T FORGET YOUR APPLICATION FEE AND SNAPSHOT."

On a yellow sheet are nine statements about Satan:

1. Satan represents indulgence, instead of abstinence!
2. Satan represents vital existence, instead of spiritual pipe dreams!
3. Satan represents undefiled wisdom, instead of hypocritical self-deceit!
4. Satan represents kindness to those who deserve it, instead of love wasted on ingrates!
5. Satan represents responsibility to the responsible, instead of concern for psychic vampires!
7. Satan represents man as just another animal—sometimes better, more often worse than those that walk on all fours, who, because of his divine spiritual and intellectual development, has become that most vicious animal of all!
8. Satan represents all of the so-called sins, as they all lead to physical, mental, or emotional gratification!
9. Satan has been the best friend the Church has ever had, as he has kept it in business all these years!

Reading the *Satanic Bible*, I found certain elements of truth which were borne out in our research of the occult, and which serve to explain the popularity of Satanism and the other occults in all their bizarre forms.

"Every practitioner of witchcraft is convinced that he or she is doing the 'right' thing," LaVey claims in the *Satanic Bible*.

He also confirms in his bible the role of sex in witch-craft:

"The most important asset to the modern witch is her ability to be alluring, or to utilize glamour.

"The word 'fascination' has a similarly occult origin.

"Fascination was the term applied to the evil eye. To fix a person's gaze, in other words, fascinate, was to curse them with the evil eye. Therefore, if a woman had the ability to fascinate men, she was regarded as a witch."

The *Satanic Bible* instructs witches and warlocks to develop the "command to look" in order to attract and hold a person's attention. Women should use sex appeal, sentiment, or wonder as part of her "look," therefore being able to manipulate people simply because they are fearful of the consequences should they not do as she asks.

Men, in order to be "successful warlocks," are instructed to find their proper "look" in one of three categories. LaVey recommends that handsome or sexually appealing men use sex, that older men take on a "wizard" or sentimental appearance. The third type would be the man who presents a "sinister or diabolic appearance," like LaVey.

The idea that willingness to participate in sex orgies is a prerequisite for becoming a Satanist is "far from the truth," states LaVey. "In fact, opportunists who have no deeper interest in Satanism than merely the sexual aspects are emphatically discouraged."

Nonetheless, LaVey states that "Satanism condones any type of sexual activity which properly satisfies your individual desires—be they heterosexual, homosexual, bi-sexual, or even asexual, if you choose.

"Satanism also sanctions any fetish or deviation which will enhance your sex life, as long as it involves no one who does not wish to be involved."

Much has been written about the so-called "new morality," but little has been said by its advocates about the staggering toll it has taken in unwanted pregnancies, abortions, venereal disease, divorces, and broken homes. Those who participate in extramarital and premarital sex, or in deviate sexual practices, seldom have any idea of the high cost of their foolish indulgences.

The "new morality" is nothing more than the old immorality, and the scriptural truths regarding sexual relations are as true today as when they were first handed down. Modern man has chosen to exercise his rebelliousness against God, and society as a whole pays the final price as the morally weak turn to idle sexual pursuits in the name of fun and recreation.

There is no sexual liberation in breaking our Lord's commandments. The only liberation for mankind is in knowing the meaning of the love of Jesus Christ.

There are three types of rituals used in the Church of Satan:

    (A) To summon one for lustful purpose or establish a sexually gratifying situation.

    (B) To insure help or success for one who has your sympathy or compassion (including yourself).

    (C) To cause the destruction of an enemy.

In the sexual rite, the Satanist is instructed to "leave the area of the altar and remove yourself to a place which will be most conducive to the working of the respective ritual." Any means of achieving satisfaction is advocated.

For the success rite, the Satanist is to remain close to the altar and mentally picture the person to be helped.

To cause the destruction of an enemy, LaVey suggests that after forming a mental picture of the victim, the Satanist stick pins or nails into a doll representing the victim. The doll may be cloth, wax, wood, vegetable matter, or just about anything.

Other acts include "the creation of graphic imagery depicting the method of your victim's destruction, drawings, paintings, etc; the creation of a vivid literary description of your victim's ultimate end; and a detailed soliloquy directed at the intended victim, describing his torments and annihilation.

"Intense, calculated hatred and disdain should accompany this step of the ceremony," states the bible, "and no attempt should be made to stop this step until the expended energy results in a state of relative exhaustion on the part of the magician."

If requests are written, they are read aloud by the priest and then burned in the flames of a candle. "Shemhamforash!" and "Hail Satan!" is said after each request.

Devices used in a satanic ritual include black robes or all black clothing for men, and "garments which are sexually suggestive" for women. "Amulets bearing the sign of Baphomet or the traditional pentagram of Satan are worn by all participants."

The robes worn by male participants may be cowled or hooded and may cover the face.

"The purpose in covering the face is to allow the participant freedom to express emotion in the face without concern. It also lessens distraction on the part of one participant toward another," the *Satanic Bible* states.

"Black is chosen for the attire in the ritual chamber because it is symbolic of the Powers of Darkness. Sexually appealing clothing is worn by women for the purpose of stimulating the emotions of the male participants."

Because Satanism is a religion of the flesh rather than of the spirit, an altar of flesh—usually a nude woman—is used in satanic ceremonies. The woman is used because "woman is the natural passive receptor, and represents the earth mother," according to their bible.

Above the altar hangs an inverted pentagram, a five-pointed star, with two of the points up and three pointing down. Inside the pentagram is the symbolic drawing of a goat. At various times it has been called the Goat of Mendes, The Goat of a Thousand Yound, The Black Goat, The Judas Goat, or The Scapegoat.

Implications from the term "Judas Goat" are immediately apparent. The Bible speaks of a scapegoat only in the sixteenth chapter of Leviticus. While theologians differ on its exact meaning, some of them consider the scapegoat an evil spirit, based on the eighth verse. In this verse, Aaron is instructed to cast lots upon two goats which have been selected, "one lot for the Lord and the other lot for the scapegoat."

Regardless of the term, the goat symbol used by Satanists is also known as the Symbol of Baphomet, which was used by the Knights Templar to represent Satan.

Black candles are used in the rituals for power and success for the participants of the ritual. A white candle is used for destruction of enemies.

A bell is used to mark both the beginning and end of the ritual, and its tonal quality "should be loud and penetrating rather than soft and tinkling," the *Satanic Bible* states.

A chalice, made of anything but gold, is used, and filled with "elixir," or whatever drink is most stimulating and pleasing to the palate. The elixir, according to those who have participated in the ritual, is usually 100 proof whiskey.

A sword is used by the priest as the symbol of aggressive force. The sword is held by the priest and is used to point towards the symbol of Baphomet during the Invocation to Satan.

A phallus (pagan fertility symbol) made from plaster, wood, clay, or wax is used in organized group rituals, as a symbol which represents generation, virility, and aggression.

The phallus is held in both hands of one of the priest's assistants and methodically shaken twice towards each cardinal point of the compass for the "benediction of the house."

A gong is used to call "upon the forces of Darkness." Finally, parchment or plain paper is used by the participants to write their messages which are given to the priest.

LaVey is careful to note that "the usual assumption is that the satanic ceremony or service is always called a Black Mass. A Black Mass is *not* the magical ceremony practiced by Satanists. The Satanist would only employ the use of a Black Mass as a form of psychodrama."

"Furthermore, a Black Mass does not necessarily imply that the performers of such are Satanists. A Black Mass is essentially a parody on the religious service of the Roman Catholic Church, but can be loosely applied to a satire in any religious ceremony," according to LaVey.

LaVey seems to be playing with words, for there are many close similarities between the Black Mass and the rituals of the Church of Satan. In fact, he states that "any ceremony considered a Black Mass must effectively shock and outrage, as this seems to be the measure of its success."

Their ritual is certainly a shock and outrage to Christians, and should be to any person in his right mind. I wonder what it could take to shock and outrage a Satanist?

As the reader can see, the Church of Satan is the antithesis of Christianity. Its beliefs are an outrage, blasphemy to those who know Jesus Christ.

It is easy for anyone with a smattering of decency to see the selfishness, lust, power, and hateful overtones of this so-called "church."

If Christians see the obvious flaws in Satanism and readily reject LaVey's self-indulgent, anti-Christ philosophy, why should they be concerned about the growth and increasing popularity of this force?

Concerned citizens and Christians should be alerted about the satanic influences for several reasons.

1. Satanism poses a threat to the values that have long held the fabric of our society together. These are the characteristics known as love of our fellowman, belief in God, abstinence from overindulgence, moderation, fair play, respect for the rights of others, liberty, and freedom. When one embraces the selfish philosophy of the Satanist church, one is rejecting those positive values that come with humanitarian respect for others.

Improving the lot of mankind on this earth is impossible when we think only of ourselves. Our Christian commitment and Christ's love teaches us that we must love others as ourselves. A life that is based solely on "me first" quickly resorts to a low form of barbarism.

2. Satanism's growth is a sign of the decay that threatens to cripple the moral fiber of any strong nation.

America was built on individualism, but not the kind of individualism proposed by LaVey.

America's forefathers made no bones about their belief in God and their dependence upon the Almighty to forge ahead in building the greatest nation on earth.

To allow the philosophy of Satanism to permeate society is to poison the body of the nation. Satanism promotes a brand of permissiveness which is inconsistent with promoting responsibility for the improvement of the individual or his fellow man.

3. Satanism attracts and encourages antisocial behavior. While LaVey may deny that his church would encourage anyone to murder or wrong others, nonetheless

its rituals encourage hate. Nothing or little is said about the real power of love.

The mentally unbalanced who follow Satanism frequently go off the deep end and commit crimes, as reported elsewhere in this book.

Practicing Satanists take glee in attacking Christians and the institutions that they stand for in America. The challenge of Satanism is a great one to Christians everywhere. Every act of selfishness practiced by Satanists requires that Christians everywhere openly express the love of Jesus Christ, not only in words, but in deeds.

14

Jeane Dixon—Angel of Light

In more than 300 American cities today, thousands of newspaper readers will open their papers and read such advice as "Diversify your efforts, " "Don't confide personal affairs today," or "Luck is indicated for today."

Then, disquieted or comforted as the case may be, they will launch into their day aiming for the goals which Jeane Dixon has pinpointed for them in her daily astrological column.

Despite biblical warnings against astrology, this Washington real estate woman has become a powerful figure in the American occult scene today.

Gracious and charming, embraced in high Washington social and political circles, Mrs. Dixon gained renown as the "prophetess" who predicted the assassination of President John F. Kennedy.

Mrs. Dixon claims that her widely publicized prophetic power is a gift from God. She attends mass every morning and claims to be a devout Catholic. Some of the leading figures on the evangelical scene in America, as well, are numbered among her personal friends.

What is the truth about this woman who has become world famous for her powers to foretell and whose books have sold more than three million copies?

The truth is that, however charming she may be and however often she may attend church, the practices and teachings of Jeane Dixon are diametrically opposed to the *Holy Bible* which warns against palmistry, witchcraft, and astrology.

In 2 Corinthians 11:13 we read that Satan himself is transformed into an angel of light, and in 1 Timothy 4:1 we learn that "the Spirit explicitly says that in the later times some will fall away from the faith, paying attention to deceitful spirits and doctrines of demons."

Deceitful spirits are not something that cause you to plunge immediately into the gory depths of Satanism, but are rather those spirits which entice you step by step, inch by inch, away from God's Word and right belief into false paths.

The Bible clearly denounces the sins of astrology and fortune telling without any concessions to Jeane Dixon's outward manifestations of good intentions, social connections, and evangelical friends.

If it is necessary to take up the "sword of the Spirit" against the undisguised forces of Satan, it is even more needful to expose those practices which are more hidden in nature but which nevertheless entice unsuspecting men and women into the clutches of evil practices.

Isaiah 47:12-14 says:

> Stand fast now in your spells
> And in your many sorceries
> With which you have labored from your youth;
> Perhaps you will be able to profit,
> Perhaps you may cause trembling.
>
> You are wearied with your many counsels,
> Let now the astrologers,
> Those who prophesy by the stars,
> Those who predict by the new moons,
> Stand up and save you from what will come upon you.
>
> Behold, they have become like stubble,
> Fire burns them;
> They cannot deliver themselves from the power of the flame.

In addition to astrology, Mrs. Dixon also practices sooth-saying.

By no stretch of the imagination can her predictions be aligned with biblical gifts of prophecy, for she makes use of such occult items as crystal balls and black cats. She attributes at least part of her power to a blood-chilling vision she had of a snake, the very symbol of evil.

Known as the "Washington Seeress," Mrs. Dixon has been credited with correctly predicting the deaths of John F. and Robert Kennedy, Martin Luther King, and the three astronauts on the launching pad at Cape Kennedy, as well as other events which have made headlines in recent years.

The truth is that many of her so-called fulfilled prophecies were very general in scope, and her predictions which have missed are countless. The misses are largely unpublicized.

Many critics do not give Mrs. Dixon credit for her prediction of President Kennedy's assassination. According to *Parade Magazine*, May 13, 1966, she made the following reference to the assassination seven years prior to the event: "As to the 1960 election, Mrs. Dixon thinks it will be dominated by labor and won by a Democrat. But he will be assassinated or die in office, though not necessarily in his first term."

Critics claim her statement was a generality in which the election was not dominated by labor, nor did she name the Democrat who would be elected. The president could die of natural causes and still the prophecy be declared fulfilled.

The prophecy concerning the death of a president in office at that time was not illogical since one out of every four presidents has died in office at approximately fifteen to twenty year intervals.

William Henry Harrison died in 1841 as a result of pneumonia; Zachary Taylor in 1850 from typhus; Abraham Lincoln, James Garfield, and William McKinley were assassinated in 1865, 1881, and 1901, respectively; Warren G. Harding died of an illness, perhaps ptomaine poisoning and bronchial pneumonia, in 1923; Franklin Roosevelt died of cerebral hemorrhage in 1945, and Kennedy was shot in 1963.

Woodrow Wilson and Dwight Eisenhower were critically ill during their terms of office, and attempts on the life of presidents have been a routine problem for the past seventy years. Actually there is an indication that her forecast was somewhat more pinpointed, for in the May 13, 1956, issue of *Parade Magazine*, reporters quoted her as saying a blue-eyed democrat elected in 1960 would be assassinated. Yet James Bjornstad in his book, *Twentieth Century Prophecy*, says that in August, 1960, Mrs. Dixon predicted a Nixon victory.

Rene Noorbergen, who worked with Mrs. Dixon on *My Life and Prophecies*, wrote in the *Insight Magazine* of June 8, 1971, that four hours before Kennedy died, Jeane Dixon told a companion that "this is the day it will happen."

Though Noorbergen had a falling out with Jeane after he helped write her book, his *Insight* article credited her with amazingly accurate predictions concerning the deaths of Dr. Martin Luther King, Senator Robert Kennedy, John Foster Dulles, Winston Churchill, Mahatma Ghandi, and Dag Hammarskjold. He also listed a number of predictions she made which failed to materialize.

Despite an amazing number of generalities and misses in her predictions, Jeane's books have sold fantastically well.

Noorbergen, in his *Insight* article, said that her astrology column appeared in more than 300 newspapers, a figure also given in the July 12, 1972 issue of the Jamestown, New York, *Post Journal.* Neither Mrs. Dixon's office nor the *Chicago Tribune-New York Times* Syndicate which distributes the column would comment on this figure.

Neither would the Dixon office nor William Morrow and Company, publishers of her books, comment on a report in the *Southern Cross*, August 19, 1971, edition, that her books had sold more than three million copies.

Her business connections and the scope of her printed material no doubt have given her considerable leverage in what some view as a one-woman empire, wielding immense power in Washington in real estate, in banking interests, and over personal lives.

Her influential circle of acquaintances is evidenced by the generous sprinkling of name-dropping found in her books. These include influential Washington officials and top entertainment personalities.

The names of Henry Ford, General and Mrs. Jimmy Doolittle, Myrna Loy and Robert Montgomery, Harry Truman, Franklin Roosevelt, Sam Rayburn, and Joseph E. Davies roll easily from her typewriter.

The scope includes such personalities as Eric Johnson, former president of the National Chamber of Commerce and later president of the Motion Picture Association of America, to Mary Goldsmith, an executive at the International Teamsters' Union headquarters.

Through frequent appearances at embassy parties, she has developed friendships with numerous ambassadors, their wives, and aides.

Many of these contacts could of course give valuable clues to events taking place not only in Washington but around the world.

Mrs. Dixon has remained a controversial figure in many quarters. Many have wondered if she is a true prophetess or a "put on" and whether her predictions are to be trusted.

To present a portrait of this lady, we have consulted Mrs. Dixon herself, as well as her books, her friends, and her acquaintances.

According to Ruth Montgomery's book *A Gift of Prophecy*, the "prophetess" was born Jeane Pinckert in the Wisconsin lumbering village of Medford in 1918, just before the armistice that ended the first World War. Her father had amassed a small fortune in Germany enabling him to retire at the age of forty-five and move his wife and six children to Santa Rosa, California.

Mr. Pinckert became interested in the nomadic gypsies who roamed the countryside. After he had come in contact with a gypsy woman who was camping on horticulturist Luther Burbank's estate, he suggested that the impressionable eight-year-old Jeane be taken to see her. The gypsy woman reportedly took Jeane's hands, turned them over and reacted with astonishment.

"This little girl is going to be very famous," the gypsy allegedly said. "She will be able to foresee worldwide changes, because she is blessed with the gift for prophecy. Never have I seen such palm lines!"

What the gypsy woman supposedly saw in Jeane's left hand was the star of David and other lines which symbolized

131

her gift for prophecy. The gypsy then gave Jeane her crystal ball to keep. The story is told that Jeane took one look into her new toy and began to see pictures as though she were watching a television screen.

Magician Milbourne Christopher, in his book *ESP, Seers and Psychics*, states that Mrs. Dixon "has since explained that if she knows the astrological sign under which someone was born she can find the future in a special segment of her crystal. Some signs are tuned in better at the center of the sphere, others are read to the left, right, above or below."

He quoted Julius Zancig, an earlier user of the crystal ball, as saying that a doorknob could be used just as effectively and that if one has a lively imagination the scenes conjured up can be "quite entertaining." He warned, however, that prolonged staring produces headaches. He also claimed that some psychiatrists take it as a sign of trouble on a person's horizon if he really believes he can see the future in a crystal ball.

Anyway, with encouragement from her mother, Jeane played with her crystal ball and made predictions for family and friends. The family moved to Los Angeles when Jeane was nine, and the child quickly built a reputation in her neighborhood as a "seeress."

Her unusual powers attracted strangers to the house seeking readings. Among these was an obscure actress named Marie Dressler who told Jeane she was having no success in acting and was thinking of opening a boarding house.

Jeane looked into her crystal ball, and according to Ruth Montgomery's book, *A Gift of Prophecy*, it "lighted up like the Fourth of July sparkler, but shooting off from the sparkler were hundred and thousands of dollar bills." Jeane interpreted this to to mean that Miss Dressler would become a star and earn a lot of money. She counseled the actress to continue her career.

After Miss Dressler received top billing on movie marquees across the country, she supposedly told people that if it had not been for "little Jeane Pinckert," she would have abandoned the theatre.

Even before Jeane was a teenager, some of the biggest

names in Hollywood were coming to her house for readings. This early success and association with the city's many unusual inhabitants whetted her appetite for acting and singing.

Among the friends of Jeane's parents was Jimmy Dixon, a bachelor in his thirty's who operated an automobile agency and moved with a fun-loving Hollywood crowd. Dixon impressed twelve-year-old Jeane Pinckert, whose admiration for him quickly turned to puppy love. Even though her age was unsuitable, Jeane was heartbroken when Dixon married someone else.

When she was twenty-one, Jeane ran into Dixon again at the Santa Anita race track and learned that he had been divorced.

"This is the future Mrs. Dixon," Dixon said as he introduced Jeane to his companion. After a five-week, whirlwind courtship with dates chaperoned by Dixon's mother, the couple married.

It is not clear if young Jeane Pinckert consulted her crystal ball on her decision to marry Dixon, for she returned the five carat diamond engagement ring twice before they finally married.

Jeane supposedly received ecclesiastical dispensation from the Catholic Church in order to marry a divorced man, and a priest performed the marriage ceremony in San Diego.

Jeane and Jim's mother became devoted to each other, and when the elder Mrs. Dixon died, she left her estate to Jeane rather than to her own children.

When Jimmy went to Detroit to work on defense projects as the war in Europe began, Jeane went along. There she met Henry Ford and allegedly prophesied the death of his son and the lapse in production of Ford autos. This lapse naturally occurred as war production occupied all motor assembly plants.

After the United States entered the war, the Dixons moved to Washington, D.C., where Dixon was involved in handling real estate for the government.

As a volunteer for the Home Hospitality Committee, Jeane would give "readings" for servicemen and convalescents from army and navy hospitals. She also "read" for various legislators and diplomats.

Because of Jimmy's extensive wartime dealings, his background in real estate, and the many friends they had made in Washington high society, the Dixons decided to remain in the capital after the war.

By the early 1960s Jeane's fame had spread to New York, and she began writing a syndicated daily horoscope column which brought additional fame and fortune.

In 1965 and 1966 Jeane Dixon skyrocketed to national prominence with the publication of the book *A Gift of Prophecy*, by Washington newswoman Ruth Montgomery. In July, 1965, a condensed version of the book appeared in *Reader's Digest* under the title *The Crystal Ball*. From August to December of 1965, the book went through twelve printings. Overnight, the name and predictions of Jeane Dixon "caught on." By the twenty-seventh printing of the paperback edition in September, 1970, it had sold more than two million copies. Mrs. Dixon has been much in demand as a speaker around the nation, commanding fees up to $5,000 an appearance, according to Harvey Katz in the *Washingtonian*, spring, 1970.

In September of 1969 a second book, *My Life and Prophecies*, was released, authored by Rene Noorbergen, a veteran free-lance psychic writer who lives in the Washington area. He has also written David Bubar's book entitled *You Are Psychic*.

Mrs. Dixon, reportedly at odds with her previous writers, is said to have used a third ghost writer for her recent book, *Reincarnation and Prayers to Live By*.

While history was proving many of Mrs. Dixon's predictions accurate, her former ghost writer, Noorbergen, and other writers were carefully weighing her other prophecies.

"In judging modern day psychics and prophets I first try to establish their P.A.Q. (Prophetic Accuracy Quotient), based on their 'hits and misses,' " wrote Noorbergen in the June 8, 1971, *Insight* magazine. "In the case of Jeane Dixon she has had her share of misses."

James Bjornstad, in his book *Twentieth Century Prophecy*, compared both Edgar Cayce (another twentieth century "prophet") and Jeane Dixon with the standards set forth in the *Bible* for prophets of God. Bjornstad makes some interesting observations in regard to Jeane Dixon's predictions.

"In her column in the *Herald News*, January 27, 1963, Jeane Dixon predicted that the Democratic nomination for the presidency of that year would go to President Lyndon B. Johnson. This prophecy was never fulfilled," writes Bjornstad. President Johnson backed out of that race, leaving Hubert Humphrey to take up the challenge.

Regarding the 1964 election, she stated that Walter Reuther would actively seek the presidency and that he would receive the Democratic nomination with Richard Nixon as his Republican opponent. Neither Reuther nor Nixon ran in that campaign.

Just prior to the 1972 Democratic National Convention, Mrs. Dixon was quoted in the Jamestown, New York, *Post-Journal* of July 12 as predicting that George McGovern would not be in the running. McGovern, of course, was the easy winner of the Democratic nomination and was most assuredly "in the running."

In *A Gift of Prophecy*, Ruth Montgomery writes of Jeane Dixon's prediction that Red China would plunge into war over Quemoy and Matsu in October of 1958. That failed to happen.

The New York Daily News, on January 1, 1953, contains a Dixon prediction that President Eisenhower would appoint General Douglas MacArthur to an important post in his administration, probably an ambassadorship. This was another miss.

Bjornstad goes on to say that at one point in her prophetic ministry, Jeane Dixon predicted that "World War III would break out in 1958."

She also predicted that Red China would be admitted to the United Nations in 1959, something which did not occur until 1971.

Many of her predictions on Red China have been wrong. Of President Nixon's trip to Peking she said, "I do get very strongly the possibility of bodily harm or injury. I get that attempts to harm the President will come from two sources—Chinese secret societies now being revived inside Red China, and dissatisfied but ambitious military personnel in the Red Chinese Army. Their aim will be to dramatize China's internal situation and draw world attention.

"The greatest danger to President Nixon will be upon his arrival at the airport . . . especially when he enters the vehicle which will take him into the city of Peking.

"President Nixon will be widely misquoted and misunderstood during this trip."

Millions of Americans who were able to watch the Peking visit on television are well aware that none of these predictions came to pass.

Bjornstad's research shows that "Jeane Dixon was asked on May 7, 1966, at the Hancock Auditorium of the University of Southern California how long the current war in Vietnam would last. Her answer was that the war would end in ninety days, "but not on our terms."

In *My Life and Prophecies* Jeane Dixon stated that Bishop Pike "will eventually become successful in another field," and that he would be "absolutely uncanny—in fact, a genius—as a medical diagnostician. Fortunately, I see that he will lose his frustrations in his new vocation."

Bishop Pike died in an Israeli desert before the book was in the bookstores.

As Noorbergen points out, "There is practically no limit to the number of unfulfilled predictions made by Jeane Dixon."

One reason Mrs. Dixon's percentage of "hits" may be higher than that of other forecasters is because she is living and working among a Washington crowd who have access to much confidential information, as pointed out earlier.

Her 1972 predictions are full of generalities and statements which could be made from knowledge gained through the *Washington Post*, social circles, government real estate clients, diplomatic contacts, and legislative sources.

Research writer Stephan A. Schwartz states in *Washingtonian* magazine that "oil billionaire H. L. Hunt sometimes calls Jeane two or three times a week, and while on the phone, may pass on inside information which Jeane is able to use in her columns and speeches."

How the energetic Jeane Dixon has time for her speaking

engagements, real estate business, answering letters, writing books, attending to a foundation she heads, and her other activities, including writing a daily syndicated newspaper column, is something that puzzles many.

Insight as to how Mrs. Dixon views herself may be gained from a conversation reported by Noorbergen in which she referred to a meeting with a spiritual psychic.

"In a talk I had with Mr. Ghandi," she is quoted as saying, "I discussed my work and my future. He feels as I do that I am just at the beginning of my destiny. There will come a time when all of humanity will flock to my feet and ask me for help and spiritual guidance."

The psychic referred to is M. K. Ghandi, not to be confused with the late Indian Hindu leader. Plans for Ghandi to teach Mrs. Dixon astrology based on mathematical calculations failed to materialize.

Mrs. Dixon reportedly uses her crystal ball for astrological forecasts rather than the stars.

At a Hollywood, California, Chamber of Commerce dinner in November, 1971, she defined astrology as a science. "It is also a glorious key to the pattern energy of the Infinite," she explained, "and this cosmic force is God's expression of His divine plan that can be seen in the various stars and planets that comprise our universe. And this energy, this pattern of cosmos is from everlasting to everlasting. Astrology takes the stars from our eyes and puts them into our lives."

She could not be further from the truth on both counts, for any astronomer or aerospace scientist in the world will testify that astrology is not a science. Also, God's Word in the *Bible* instructs people not to follow the stars, such as in the passage quoted from Isaiah earlier.

When King Nebuchadnezzar was seeking advice from astrologers and soothsayers, as related in the second chapter of the book of Daniel, Daniel himself put his finger on just who has knowledge of the future.

In Daniel 2:27, Daniel says, "As for the mystery about which the king has inquired, neither wise men, conjurers, magicians, nor diviners are able to declare it to the king."

Then in the next verse, Daniel pointed to the One who is able to give the answers when he said, "However, there is a God in heaven who reveals mysteries. . . ." He it is to Whom we should turn for direction rather than to other means He has expressly forbidden.

A pertinent question which must be faced is whether or not Mrs. Dixon's practice of astrology is compatible with the position of the Catholic Church. She claims to be a devout Catholic and contends that there is no conflict between the practice of astrology and the moral guidelines of the Roman Catholic Church.

The Oakland, California, *Catholic Voice* in its issue of November 11, 1971, pointed out in an editorial that "Occultism is a serious threat to religion, and it is diametrically opposed to the fundamental principles of religion."

Listing such occults as Tarot, I Ching, astrology, zodiac, and witches' covens, the editorial declares that "all these deny the reality of a personal God, and set up a priority on power and control." It added that Christians view these manifestations with alarm.

Concerning specific doctrine, the question comes under the study of moral theology. One of the Catholic Church's best known authorities on moral theology is Father Edwin Healy who has taught at Loyola University and in Rome.

He states that the church teaches against occults under the first commandment: "You shall have no other gods before Me." (Exodus 20:3)

Father Healy outlines the Catholic Church's teaching on this area in his book entitled, *Moral Guidance*, published by Loyola University Press in 1942, which is still the contemporary guideline on the matter. He spends thirty pages talking about "Forbidden Forms of Worship" which include idolatry, divination, fortune telling, crystal gazing, astrology, wrong uses of hypnotism, dream omens, Ouija boards, palmistry, mental telepathy, spiritism, and any other superstitious practices.

Concerning astrology, Father Healy said that astrologers reading the free future in the stars try to adorn themselves with divine attributes. "It is against the doctrine of free will, for it leads to a fatalistic view," he wrote, and added, "Astrologers contend that all things happen according to a predetermined fate which can be read in one's horoscope. Hence no matter how one tries to avoid

138

this or that, his attempts are in vain because his fate has been sealed years ago by the stars. It is against belief in divine providence for according to astrology, God is not guiding us and helping us by his grace through the trials of temptation. If we were to judge by what astrologers teach, prayer would be fruitless and without purpose. The church has always condemned the false teaching of judicial astrology."

Father Healy, having made the Catholic Church's position clear on astrology, goes on to point out that in all forms of divination a person can call on Satan directly or indirectly.

"Divination is the art of learning hidden events, particularly future hidden events that depend upon either expressly or passively appealing to Satan. But what about this passive appeal to Satan? You don't do it in so many expressed words, but by virtue of the circumstances where divine enlightment cannot reasonably be expected, we go ahead and try to discover hidden knowledge through means that are naturally inadequate for furnishing such knowledge. For example, a naturally inadequate means by which we try to learn future events is by gazing into crystal globes. So the church has always been opposed to all of this."

Despite these and similar teachings by respected Catholic theologians, Jeane Dixon continues to insist that she is a devout Catholic and adheres to the rituals of the church.

She dedicated her book *Reincarnation and Prayers to Live By* to Reverend Father Stephen Hartdegen, O.F.M., who was an editor-in-chief of the contemporary Catholic version of the *Bible* and is associated with Holy Name College in Washington, D.C.

Reincarnation is another belief of Mrs. Dixon's which is at odds with the *Holy Bible.* Those who believe in reincarnation believe that after death a person is born back into this life as another person.

Biblical teaching is that a person lives one life here, and after death, the soul goes to either heaven or hell, depending on what that person has done about acknowledging Jesus Christ as Savior. Hebrews 9:27 says, "It is appointed for men to die once, and after this comes judgment."

Our researchers spoke several times to Mrs. Dixon

during preparation of this book. Once she was asked point blank if she knew about the biblical passages with prohibitions against sorcery and astrology, such as Deuteronomy 18:10-12, which says, "There shall not be found among you anyone who makes his son or his daughter to pass through the fire, one who uses divination, one who practices witchcraft, or one who interprets omens, or a sorcerer, or one who casts a spell, or a medium, or a spiritist, or one who calls up the dead. For whoever does these things is detestable to the Lord; and because of these detestable things the Lord you God will drive them out before you."

Jeane Dixon's answer was as follows: "Well, what is a sorcerer?" Then she explained the other part of the question. "To me, astrology is a science to a point. And beyond that point to be psychic helps an awful lot. I know the Bible says something about astrology, but I don't consider myself a fortuneteller at all. My gift is from God, given to me for the benefit of others. I bring good luck to people."

The Scriptures throughout are clear that there is no such thing as "luck." God is sovereign and reigns in the affairs of men. Man, of course, is equipped with a free will which enables him to make moral choices, but it is God who brings to pass the consequences of man's acts.

Psalms 37:23 says, "The steps of a man are established by the Lord." Verses four and five of that Psalm say, "Delight yourself in the Lord; And He will give you the desires of your heart. Commit your way to the Lord, trust also in Him, and He will do it."

The blessings and mercies of God are divinely bestowed. They have nothing to do with luck.

Mrs. Dixon's ideas are clearly out of line with Bible prophets who spoke as "they were moved by the Holy Ghost."

Her use of astrology, a crystal ball to receive visions and telepathic messages, and her meditation sessions with her black cat, tie in instead with soothsayers and magicians. Mrs. Dixon claims her meditations with "Mike the MagiCat" often open the way for her to receive inspired visions.

Even though Mrs. Dixon believes in the power of Jesus, according to writer Noorbergen, she believes there are innumerable channels and "each must find the right one for him."

Noorbergen concludes that, "A careful comparison between the life and prophecies of Jeane Dixon and the biblical tests of a prophet can leave little doubt in one's mind as to what she is."

We have come into contact with many Christians who have been ignorant of what God has to say on the subject of soothsayers.

A friend of mine preached just recently in a Northern California city on this subject and afterwards a deacon of the church came and told him that he had been practicing astrology. After being enlightened about biblical teaching on the subject, he went home and tore up his astrology charts. This is a course of action I heartily recommend to anyone who has become involved in this devilish practice.

Some people regard astrology and fortune telling as "fun," but like everything contrary to God's Word, it has the sting of death in it. Also, it can become a very real bondage to those who begin by becoming even slightly involved in this activity.

I've known businessmen who wouldn't transact business at a certain time because the stars were "not favorable."

I've come to the place that I won't even read fortune cookies that come with meals in Chinese restaurants, not even as a game.

I choose to get my direction for each day from the book that never makes a mistake, the *Bible*, and through direct communion with God in daily devotional prayer.

I know of no "luck" which can in any way compete with the blessings of God! Listen to what He says in the ninety-first Psalm:

He who dwells in the shelter of the Most High
Will abide in the shadow of the Almighty.
I will say to the Lord, "My refuge and my fortress,
My God, in whom I trust!"
For it is He who delivers you from the snare of the
        trapper,
And from the deadly pestilence.
He will cover you with His pinions,
And under His wings you may seek refuge;
His faithfulness is a shield and bulwark.

You will not be afraid of the terror by night,
Or of the arrow that flies by day;
Of the pestilence that stalks in darkness,
Or of the destruction that lays waste at noon.
A thousand may fall at your side,
And ten thousand at your right hand;
But it shall not approach you.
You will only look on with your eyes,
And see the recompense of the wicked.
For you have made the Lord, my refuge,
Even the Most High, your dwelling place.
No evil will befall you,
Nor will any plague come near your tent.

For He will give His angels charge concerning you,
To guard you in all your ways.
They will bear you up in their hands,
Lest you strike your foot against a stone.
You will tread upon the lion and cobra,
The young lion and the serpent you will trample down.

Because he has loved Me, therefore I will deliver him;
I will set him securely on high, because he has
      known My name.
He will call upon Me, and I will answer him;
I will be with him in trouble;
I will rescue him, and honor him.
With a long life I will satisfy him,
And let him behold My salvation.

15

Charge-A-Hex

If you are short of ready cash but long on enemies, then you may hex somebody and charge it!

That may sound funny, but it is something which can be done, according to signs on voodoo shops in the Miami area. These shops, or botanicas, abound in areas of the United States where voodoo is common, such as in the deep South.

They boldly display Master Charge signs and invitations to use their layaway plans. Thus, potions and charms may be obtained to work magic against enemies "on the cuff."

In the "Little Havana" area of Miami there are more than twenty of these botanicas featuring a variety of items from jinx-removing soap to powdered bats.

These shops come in various sizes and atmospheres. One on S.W. 12 Avenue is freshly painted and air-conditioned and features plenty of free parking. Another, only a block from the downtown federal building, is dark and dingy and heavy with the smell of incense. In Hialeah, there is one located in the rear of a pet store.

Among items offered are voodoo dolls, Luck Shampoo, Love Spray, Fast Luck Spray, Drawing Power Spray, fish heads, whale teeth, medium's alcohol, money blessing powder, protection lotions, cat skulls, a wolf's eye, graveyard dust, and a variety of other items used by the superstitious and believers in voodoo.

Many of the items aren't really what they are labeled. The graveyard dust, for instance, might actually come from a graveyard, but it is usually the powdered leaves of mullein which have a musty odor frequently associated with cemeteries.

Many of the botanica owners deny they have anything to do with voodoo or witchcraft, but after they become friendly, they will refer you to a "doctor" who can help you, presuming of course, that they can sell you the proper supplies after the doctor has given you a "prescription."

A "prescription" may call for obtaining a voodoo doll costing anywhere from $1.50 for a simple black and red cloth doll to a more elaborately dressed one for $5. The doll, to be effective, must be dressed in the color of clothing worn by the person you wish to harm.

You simply write the name of the person on a piece of paper and then stick it beneath the doll's clothing above the heart. Then pins are stuck into the doll and are said to cause pain and sickness in the other person.

Some "prescriptions" are prepared by "readers" of shells. Using twenty-one small, round shells, the reader casts them on a table and then studies their pattern. Based on this, a combination of herbs is prescribed to solve problems of love, business, family, and health.

Dried rats' heads, bone, and special bits of fish may also be purchased in the botanicas for voodoo rites.

Voodoo is practiced underground in many hard-core Negro ghettos, and is found in most southern states as well as on some college campuses. New York, with its large concentration of Negroes, Puerto Ricans, and Caribbeans, is rapidly emerging as the voodoo capital of America.

The word voodoo comes from the old French "vaudeaux," Antichrist cults which practiced Black Mass and used potent herbs to win the minds and bodies of followers or enemies. The male ruler of a cult is called *Papaloi*, and the female is called *Mamaloi*.

Voodoo in early America originated among Negro slaves as a protective means to scare the white overseer

144

into being more kind and, in some cases, to overpower him. At one time, voodoo was so rampant in the Deep South that authorities prohibited the importation of slaves from Martinique because these were so strongly inclined to practice voodoo.

Recently in Rio de Janeiro, Brazil, a half million devotees of voodoo spent New Year's Eve on the beaches of Rio, sacrificing chickens and sending gifts to the sea goddess Yemanja in hopes of a lucky year. While drums beat and thousands chanted, the white-robed voodoo priests waded into the water with gifts of flowers and small boats loaded with perfume, cosmetics, rum, and champagne for Yemanja.

Many Brazilians believe the sea goddess determines their fortunes for the new year. If the gifts are swept out to sea by the tide during the night, the goddess is deemed to have accepted them, and the year will be happy. If they wash ashore, it is believed they have been rejected, and the cultists prepare for a bad year.

One of the most authentic accounts of Brazilian voodoo practice was given by Otilia Pontes in a recent edition of *World Vision Magazine.**

Mrs. Pontes, the wife of a high-ranking officer in the Brazilian army, was a virtual prisoner of "Macumba," a Brazilian voodoo cult. She is now a Christian.

"Voodoo is more than superstition," she declares. "It is a real and powerful force that binds its followers in chains of fear. . . . Its devotees include people from all walks of life, the cultured and the educated as well as the lowly."

Her involvement with voodoo began in Rio after she came from the interior. She was working in a cloth factory where, during working hours, women wore a head scarf.

"One day I felt that somebody was pulling my hair. My head ached, and I felt dizzy and ill," she says. "On Wednesday and Friday the same symptoms returned. It happened on alternate days, always on Mondays, Wednesdays, and Fridays.

"The symptoms grew worse. I fainted often and could

---

* Otilia Pontes, "From Voodoo to Christ," as told to Wilson Villanova, *World Vision Magazine*, March 1969, pp. 9-11.

not work for days. This was harmful to my job in the factory. The doctors I consulted could not help me. Their treatment brought no results whatever.

"Then my boss, a voodooist, invited me to go and take treatment from Grandma Cabinda. In hope of being cured, I went with her to her 'terreiro'—the outdoor place where voodoo is practiced.

"As soon as I entered the terreiro, Grandma Cabinda, speaking through the *baba* (medium), asked for a round of applause because a great medium was entering. To the sound of drums and tambourines they sang:

> Rise Negro
> Captivity is finished by
> Sarava this day,
> Sarava our Lord.

Mrs. Pontes began to feel ill, and at the same time had a desire to dance, she says.

"I could not control myself. When the chant changed to a difficult voodoo dance in which they made gestures of throwing arrows, I arose, though bent by illness, and started dancing and smoking a cigar. The *baba* attended me, and I promised that if I was cured I would continue to frequent the terreiro.

"On Monday I returned to my work cured—and I also returned to voodoo. I was hooked," she says.

This started her difficult seven-year apprenticeship to become a priestess of the "Umbanda" line of Macumba. With Old Grandma of the Rosary as her "front guide," she practiced as a voodoo priestess for twenty-three years.

Her apprenticeship started with "obligations" that the terreiro demanded. She prepared fetishes for use as hexes in cemeteries, beaches, woods, and at crossroads. She took baths and prepared them.

"After one year I got orders from Father Xango, a powerful voodoo deity, to enter 'The Room' at Conga," she recalls. "This is a place where mediums stay to learn to be priestesses. We remained in 'The Room' for 17 days without seeing daylight. There were 50 women and girls with heads shaved. Every day we had a new cloth, different food and different baths—a total of 121 baths with 121 different herbs for purification and cure."

146

When the term was over, the *baba* brought the women out of the room to what was known as "the Four Banquets." Food and drink were of the finest quality, she says. At one point in the banquet the candidates were bled.

"The god of darkness is bloodthirsty and cruel," she says. "Every gesture the *baba* makes is part of a meaningful ritual. With a dagger she bleeds the candidate behind the ear and offers the blood in sacrifice to the gods: 'Mr. Crossbar Street,' 'Mr. Seven Caps,' and 'Mr. Velvet.' "

She had another year of obligations—hexes, small deeds, baths; then at the third stage of her apprenticeship, she learned how to make witchcraft, prayers, and sorceries.

"I knew prayers and witchcraft for all sorts of things," she says. "I could pray, for instance, to stop a hemorrhage in a person close to me or several miles away. I received the spirit of an old colored man who gave me power to open any door."

One of the most requested sorceries, she recalls, was the power to "tame husbands."

The most difficult and cruel test of all involved the sacrifice of a human life, she says.

"The *baba* called me and asked me to prepare my first hex. However, in order to do it, I had to kill my oldest son! She told me that in order to become absolute owner of my terreiro, to have power over human lives, the power of life and death, I would have to do this," Mrs. Pontes said.

"I asked for three days to think. After three days I told the *baba* that I could not do such a thing. She said I would then have to do a sorcery to make my son sick."

Her eldest son, Acyr, was seven years old. Two members of the voodoo cult went to a local cemetery in her place, and there they dedicated a diabolical "deed" to the health of Mrs. Pontes' son.

Three days later, when she arrived home, she found her mother distressed and her son, Acyr, sick.

"To heal him, I had to 'change heads.' This is an expiatory ceremony in which a person's sickness is transferred to a clean animal. I prepared a banquet in the woods. At the head of the table I put a completely black goat and my son, Acyr. He was so sick that he had to be carried like a baby. After the preparations and being cut with a dagger, I 'received' Mr. John Skull from the cemetery. He bled the goat instead of bleeding the child. I exchanged the life of the animal for my son's life."

Mrs. Pontes finally became *baba* of the Rosary. To please the Grandma of the Rosary, who was believed to be "incarnate" in Mr. Pontes, she had to drink three or four bottles of purest white rum every night and smoke both cigars and pipe.

"The rum never even made me dizzy," she recalls. "It was as if I hadn't drunk it! All these years I never went to bed before one o'clock in the morning because I had to be awake at midnight to save people from the crossroads.

"I was a beast in the form of a woman," she says, reflecting on those years. "Though I had been raised in a Christian home, I became rebellious to the point of hating the Bible and religious services. In obedience to Mr. John Skull, I could put powder in my right hand, light it with a cigar and let it explode without burning my hands and face while singing, 'Exu has two heads/ He looks at his hands with faith/ One is for Satan of hell/ The other is for Jesus of Nazareth.' "

In 1956, Mrs. Pontes' husband was transferred to Alegrete in the state of Rio Grande de Sul to be commanding officer of the military post there. In Alegrete, her youngest daughter, then eleven, came down with infectious rheumatism and hovered between life and death, unconscious for three days with an open myocardium. A spiritist doctor came to see her three times a day but he could not help her. All the voodoo practices failed.

Then a neighbor couple, Mr. and Mrs. Joao Sultan, Methodists and true believers in the power of Christ, asked permission to invite their minister, Rev. Gustavo Otto, to see the girl.

"In desperation, I agreed to the pastor's visit," Mrs. Pontes said. "He came, read the Bible, prayed, and left. Before he had reached home, Vera Lucia sat up and asked for food. The next day she was up and walking, and two weeks later she was discharged from the hospital."

Meanwhile, Rev. Almir Bahia came to Alegrete to conduct a revival campaign at the Methodist Church, and neighbors invited Mrs. Pontes to the meetings.

Mrs. Pontes' "Grandma of the Rosary" refused her permission to go and said that if she went, she would remove her from the church.

At the second meeting of the revival, while the congregation was singing "I Want to Be a Channel of Blessing," Mrs. Pontes went forward and surrendered to Christ.

"I could never tell what I felt at that moment!" she says. "I was reborn in Christ. The devil and his hosts could not conquer me. I feared them no longer. I went home and destroyed all the instruments used to deceive my neighbors."

Mrs. Pontes had discovered something I already knew—and which I hope all my readers know: *the power of God is greater than ALL the power of the enemy!*

There are many people today who think that they are hexed or under a spell. I get letters at my headquarters every week from people wanting to know how to break an evil spell or cope with hexes they think someone is putting on them.

We are in a battle called "life." It is between two powers, good or evil—God or the power of Satan. The real crux in the question is, which power is greater—Satan's influence or Jesus Christ's resurrecting, overcoming power?

That's the question. Now let me give you the answer. Christ is the answer! He is the ultimate answer to every need and able to break any evil spell that someone might have or think they have surrounding them!

The devil *cannot* stand when we take our rightful place in God and take authority over the works of darkness.

"Submit therefore to God. Resist the devil and he will flee from you." (James 4:7) That means he *has* to go when God takes over!

In an earlier chapter I recounted to you a personal encounter I had with 300 witch doctors in Haiti in 1959. These witch doctors planned to work the great assembly of people into a frenzy, tear up the platform, and kill me.

Yet the combined forces of 300 evil witch doctors were no match for the power of God. Every one of them had to hold his peace in the presence of the authority of God as exercised by His servant. Some of the leading witch doctors were converted to Christ as a result of the demonstration of God's power at that meeting.

I say to you that the combined forces of all the witch doctors in the world, all the Satanists, all the witches, yes, even all the evil spirits in existence *have to bow before the matchless power of the resurrected Christ!*

16

Spooks and Spirits

Is your dead Aunt Matilda standing beside your elbow trying to pierce the curtain between life and death and talk to you?

A lot of people think they are haunted by "ghosts" or spirits of the dead who are trying to communicate with them. Conversely, many people start out from the other direction, by trying to make contact with the dead.

The majority of the Christian world is aware of the séances conducted by the late Episcopalian Bishop James Pike in an effort to communicate with his son who had committed suicide.

Here is an area of real danger, a snare that can creep up even on evangelical ministers, to say nothing of the hundreds of spiritualist churches and ministers already existing across the nation.

The truth is that nowhere does the Scripture teach communion with the dead, but the exact opposite.

Mediums are classed along with astrologers and soothsayers in Scripture.

The *Living Bible* paraphrases Isaiah 8:19 as saying, "So why are you trying to find out the future by consulting witches and mediums? Don't listen to their whisperings and mutterings. Can the living find out the future from the dead? Why not ask your God?''

We are also told in 1 Timothy 2:5 that there is one mediator "between God and men, the man Christ Jesus.''

People *in touch with God* do not usually seek some other method of supernatural guidance. In the Old Testament it was when Saul was out of touch with God and could get no guidance from Him that he turned to mediums—to his own destruction!

Down through the ages there have been spiritists or spiritualists. The modern version got its impetus from the Fox sisters, Katy and Margaret, who in 1848 described strange happenings to convince their mother and others that they were in communication with the dead. One rap, they said, meant "yes,'' and two meant "no.'' The story spread throughout the state of New York, and people began to flock to the girls' home, hoping to get answers to their questions. For the next forty years the girls traveled throughout the world conducting séances and giving answers to all types of questions.

In 1888 the Fox sisters shocked their huge following in a large New York City auditorium with the admission that the entire thing had been a hoax from the beginning. They explained that it had started as a "joke.'' They had bounced an apple up and down on a string running through their bed mattress to produce the strange rappings.

Later they had developed better methods for producing the noises. One of these methods was demonstrated on stage that night when one of the sisters put her bare foot on a wooden stool under a spotlight and showed how she could crack the joints in her big toe to produce the rappings! She revealed that the trick had worked perfectly in the dark atmosphere of séances with wooden floors acting as sounding boards.

The rapping noises had been convincing to people starved for supernatural manifestations and word from departed loved ones. Within six years after the sisters had begun their "tricks,'' some 15,000 convinced spiritualists sent a petition to Congress seeking verification that their beliefs were scientifically sound.

Although many former spiritualists have confessed to

practicing fakery, a hard core of unrelenting spiritualists remains in existence throughout the country.

Andre Kole, an accomplished magician, has long conducted a one-man campaign to expose frauds in spiritualism. One of the features of his exposé is the history of Harry Houdini's efforts to prove or disprove communication with the dead.

Houdini had supposedly conversed with his dead mother in séances, but it remained a mystery to him and others how all her ghostly communication came through in English. Although his mother had known sixteen languages, she had not known one word of English.

Houdini recognized the fraud and started a campaign to expose fake mediums. For the next thirty years, he offered a $10,000 standing reward to anyone who could produce any type of spiritualistic phenomenon, in physical form, which he could not expose as a fraud.

During that time he is said to have attended more than 5000 séances. Before his death he stated his conclusions: He had not seen one thing he was unable to expose either as a fraud or to show simply as a psychological effect he himself was able to reproduce.

Houdini also supposedly worked out a plan with his wife. The first one of them to die would seek to communicate with the living one through a secret code known only to them. After Houdini's death, for ten years between 2 and 4 P.M. each Sunday afternoon, Mrs. Houdini would place a light over her late husband's picture. Through séances and mediums she would then try to communicate with him.

Her final séance was held at the Hotel Knickerbocker in Hollywood while other séances were being held around the world for the same purpose. For two hours eighteen people were seated round a table, praying and pleading for Houdini's spirit to come.

As at the previous séances, nothing happened. It was the tenth anniversary of Houdini's death.

"Communications with the spirit world are impossible," concluded Mrs. Houdini as she reached over and turned out the light for the last time.

Despite such efforts on the part of the Fox sisters, Kole, Houdini, and others to expose spiritualism as a hoax,

153

the cult has persisted. There are some 400 spiritualist churches in the United States with 150,000 members.

One of the greatest concentrations of spiritualist believers and mediums is to be found in Cassadaga, Florida, a community of 400 spiritualists who are members of the Southern Cassadaga Spiritualist Camp Meeting Association. For a price you are supposed to be able to communicate with the dead through a number of mediums available.

A large bulletin board on the main street of the little town lists mediums such as Wilbur Hull, D. Joseph Paquin, D.D., Catherine Pharo, and a number of others.

Signs in front of houses up and down the street read "Medium," "Clairvoyant," "Healers," or "Spiritual Advisor."

The people who live in Cassadaga take their spiritualism seriously. Visitors who come may make donations from four dollars and up to communicate with their dead loved ones, learn about the past and future, or seek advice on matters of love, family, and money.

Church services are held on Sunday at 2:30 P.M. in a plain white building. Inside, a large picture of Jesus is posted behind the lectern. We have a statement from a man who attended one of these sessions. He said there were about sixty persons present, a low attendance because it was the off-season. The speaker that day was Reverend Arthur Myers, who seemed to be about eighty years old. Attired in a red shirt with a chartreuse tie, Reverend Myers discussed life after death and the reality of conversing with the dead.

At the conclusion of the sermon, a woman, said to be one of the best spiritualists in town, called on people in the audience.

"I see your departed father behind you," she told a man sitting in the back. "Is you father in the beyond?"

The man nodded yes and she continued, "Your father is standing right in back of you, and he says that everything is O.K., and you should work hard at what you're doing and not to let down. Do you understand what I mean?"

Again he replied in the affirmative.

The woman said she "saw" loved ones and dispensed messages to other members of the audience.

Through conversing with the spiritualists, this man discovered that death, for spiritualists, is not the end, but the "unfolding of consciousness." They claim communication with the "so-called dead" is a "fact" that they have proven scientifically. The mediums are channels through which others can contact the spirit world.

Spiritualism is summed up in a brochure by Reverend Wilbur Hull, one of Cassadaga's oldest mediums. "Spiritualism is the Science, Philosophy, and Religion of continuous life, based on the demonstrated fact of communication (by means of mediumship) with those in an advanced non-physical state."

By his own admission, Hull states that "spiritualism has no creed; no rituals; no dogmatic belief ... it is the democracy of religions ... it has no 'last breath' redemption plan ... it brings hope and purpose to a confused, rebellious world; to every man a clear-cut, well-defined objective beyond physical existence."

Hull stresses that those who come to him should make an appointment because "it readies the mind for spiritual receptivity." He claims that a reading is "the serving of spirit; assisting in the alleviation of grief, the fostering of hope, guidance toward achievement, emphasizing talent, avoiding failure."

"Reach for the flow of guidance," he counsels. "Hesitate before you reject. Do not be anxious to say 'no.' *Be fair.* Expect guidance. Cooperate. Be a student."

Our researcher witnessed Reverend Hull in action. He reports that his first-hand experience would make one think that being a medium is hard work.

This is the way he described his visit:

"He [Reverend Hull] lies flat on his back in a tiny back bedroom of his house, accessible by an outside entrance. In this darkened, musty room, a white-haired man looks at you through thick lenses which magnify the size of his eyes.

"If you have not been to him before, he wants to know your background in spiritualism.

"If you want to talk to your late Uncle Joe, he will ask you for a piece of jewelry or something belonging to him. Grasping the object, Reverend Hull closes his eyes; his body begins to tremble."

"I see a large man with prominent features," he begins, speaking deliberately.

"I remembered that my uncle's nose *was* a little big . . . but then who of us *does not* have some prominent features?"

"His name starts with the letter S, I think," he continued. "Do you understand what I mean?"

"No, his name started with *J*," I replied.

"He 'saw' Uncle Joe sitting in a car next to a lady," he told me next. "Do you understand what I mean?"

"Yes, yes. I *did* see Uncle Joe sitting next to his wife in the car the last time they left my house. But then, most uncles *are* married and at sometime or other have their wives sitting beside them."

"Something happened to you in 1968, didn't it?" he demanded. "Something that changed your life?"

["That was true. However, something happens to me every year that changes my life.]

"I see a relative whose name starts with *W*. Do you understand what I mean?" he asked.

"As a matter of fact, I did have a great uncle by the name of William. And the name of my former boss was William, my cousin's first name is William. In fact, I know about four people with the first name of William—who doesn't?"

"And so I played along and analyzed his questions. They were so vague and general that 75 percent of them deserved a yes answer."

"For those who have come seeking counsel and guidance, as many bereaved and lonely people do, the powers displayed by the spiritualist seem fantastic.

"The spiritualist, of course, is a shrewd and practical observer of people. He keeps his message positive: 'Watch out for your health,' and 'you are going to come into some money soon, you had better hang on to it,' or 'watch out after dark.'

"After an hour of platitudes and generalities, the medium ran out of steam, and the séance ended."

"This takes a lot out of me," concluded the medium. "I can't turn on all the time."

"If a medium 'turns on' and tells you what you want to hear, and you *think* you have communicated with your

156

loved one, then perhaps you will make a donation. Folks have been known to contribute more than $100 to talk to Uncle Charlie or Aunt Martha.

"As I was getting ready to leave Reverend Hull's room, I heard strange noises from the bookcase."

The medium did not seem startled but explained the disturbance. "That's my intercom system," he said. "I can hear anyone approaching the house. If I want to, I can even hear conversations in the waiting room."

"I figured that was one way the medium gets the message."

Our experimenter was not particularly impressed with the psychic powers he saw at work in Cassadaga. However, traveling several miles farther to De Leon, site of the fabled "Fountain of Youth," he did run across a situation in which psychic powers seemed present.

There he heard a strange story, later confirmed by law authorities and witnesses, about two divers who disappeared in the dark caverns of a spring while skin diving one afternoon.

Larry Johnson, twenty-five, and Joe Kennick, thirty, were both certified divers. That day they stayed below long beyond the timed capacity of their aqualungs. When their failure to surface became critical, concerned onlookers called the police. Divers went down at the site with powerful lights, trying to find the pair. Their search turned up one aqualung, but no bodies.

The next day, Jim Jones, an area constable and also a diver, found Kennick's body.

That evening, Mrs. Jones was sitting at home in Deland watching a filmed account of the recovery of the body on the 9 o'clock news. Suddenly she heard a muffled voice from the wall.

"Let me out of here!"

She checked in the closet where one of the lost diver's effects had been stored, but found no one there.

Several days later, as the search for the body of Johnson continued, Mrs. Jones called a woman she knew to be a medium. At the appointed time, she went to the woman's house, and the medium, as arranged, went into a trance to try to locate Johnson's spirit.

"She described the underwater caves in De Leon spring, and told where to find the body. She also said something disastrous was going to happen the following Sunday at 1 P.M.," Mrs. Jones recalled. "When she finished talking, she said it would be a miracle if the body were ever found, and predicted it would be lost forever." Mrs. Jones related the medium's description of the caves and her prediction to her husband and the other divers.

The medium later called Mrs. Jones back and gave her a compelling warning: "Make the divers stay out of the springs until 1 P.M. Sunday!" The medium was convinced something was going to cave in.

Reluctantly, the divers heeded her warning and stayed out of the springs Saturday and Sunday.

Sunday, at 1:30 p.m., they descended again.

"The area that she said was going to cave in *had* done so," says Constable Jones.

"The other thing that bugged me was her accurate description of the caves," admitted Jim later on. "She said that there are three springs—two flowing out and one flowing back. The whirlpool formed goes around and around. She also said that the one diver had panicked and lost control; his body was jammed up in moss. She said he had white legs. Well, he was wearing white dungarees. Her description of the caves was also perfect."

This account, of course, does not endorse the medium's value. It does suggest, however, why mediums gain a following. While much of it is fake, there is also some spiritualism that is real. Many Christians who were once involved in the occult testify to the reality of supernatural manifestations "from the other side." These manifestations are the work of Satan and not of God. These spirits and the spiritualists who call on them are exposed in Scripture—despite the fact that spiritualists can and do quote the Bible, use it for responsive readings, and call on God in prayer during services and séances. As individuals they claim to be Bible-inspired followers. The basic ideas of spiritualism, however, actually deny all the fundamentals of biblical truth.

Spiritualists see Jesus as a medium who conjured up spirits and held séances with his disciples. They base their belief in spirit writing on, among other scriptures, the one describing the mighty hand of God inscribing the Ten Commandments on stone.

They describe God as "Infinite Intelligence," but they fail to present Him as a knowable Person, One who seeks to make Himself known through His Word and through His Son, Jesus Christ.

Take a look at some of the Scriptures they use, and some of the hymns they sing, based on Christian hymns, and see what they are actually doing.

Spiritualists make lavish use of existing Christian hymns but have taken great editorial liberties by changing the words completely.

In the *Spiritualist Hymnal* published by the R.D. Row Music Company of Boston exclusively for the National Spiritualist Association of Churches, there are no songs at all referring to the blood of Jesus Christ or Calvary or the atoning work of Jesus Christ.

In fact, we found the name of Jesus only twice: once in "What a Friend We Have in Jesus" and once in "O Little Town of Bethlehem."

The word "sin" appeared only once. In other songs the word "sin" was changed to "wrong" as it was in "What a Friend" where they sing "all our wrongs and griefs to bear."

This particular well-loved Christian hymn featured other changes including "Jesus knows our every weakness" to "Spirit knows our every weakness" and from "Precious Savior, still our refuge," to "Precious Spirit is our refuge."

Such songs as "I love to tell the story of unseen things" would naturally catch their fancy, but "Jesus and His glory" becomes "angels and their glory, angels and their love." Likewise, "Hand in Hand with Jesus" becomes "Hand in Hand with Angels."

A song to a tune similar to "Face to Face" has the following verse and chorus:

> Some morn the spirit friends will rap
> And I no more in doubt will be:
> But oh the joy when I shall hear
> The loving message sent to me.
>
> And I shall hear and understand,
> The message from the spirit land;

159

And I shall hear and understand
My own, my blessed angel band.

Subsequent verses contain the lines "The Odic clouds will fill the room," and "Ethereal forms will float by me."

Of particular note is a stanza evidently sung to the tune of "Let the Lower Lights be Burning" that goes as follows:

Sweetly falls the spirit's message
From the home beyond the tide
Ever do we bid thee welcome,
Dwellers from the other side.

Other songs tell you that loved ones are still near you and "try so hard to tell you," and that they will guide you "if you seek to hold communion."

In their Declaration of Principles, printed in the front cover of the hymnal, the Spiritualists "affirm that communication with the so-called dead is a fact, scientifically proven by the phenomena of Spiritualism," and also "affirm that the doorway to reformation is never closed against any human soul here or hereafter."

These precepts are expressly contradicted in the Bible. For one thing, Paul teaches us in Hebrews 9:27 that "It is appointed for men to die once, and after this comes judgment."

In His story about the rich man and Lazarus, as recounted in Luke 16:19-31, Jesus tells of the beggar and the rich man who died. One was carried by the angels to Abraham's bosom.

Of the rich man it is said, "In hell, he lifted up his eyes, being in torment." Spiritualists deny the existence of hell.

The rich man wanted Lazarus to dip his finger in water and come and touch his tongue with it "for I am in agony in this flame." The request was ungrantable, for as Abraham explained, "Between us and you there is a great chasm fixed, in order that those who wish to come over from here to you may not be able, and that none may cross over from there to us."

The rich man's next request was for Abraham to allow Lazarus to go back and warn his brothers not to come to the same place of torment. Abraham reminds him that Moses and the prophets have warned his brothers, but the rich man makes the further plea that "if someone goes to them from the dead, they will repent!"

Abraham replies, "If they do not listen to Moses and the Prophets, neither will they be persuaded if someone rises from the dead."

Nowhere does the Scripture teach of a second chance for salvation after death. Directly opposite, it warns that this life is the time to prepare for the hereafter and clearly teaches of heaven and hell.

Another statement in the Spiritualists' Declaration of Principles is that "The precept of prophecy contained in the Bible is a divine attribute proven through mediumship."

While prophecy is clearly taught in the Bible, it is not associated with spirits of the so-called dead. And mediumship, as Scriptures previously quoted in this section clearly show, was forbidden by God.

In a tract "Spiritual Phenomena in the Bible" distributed in Spiritualist churches, a list of scriptural references is given which ostensibly bear out their beliefs in materialization, spirit-writing, trumpet-speaking, levitation, and spirit communications in dreams. Most of the references could be classed as far-fetched to the Bible believer.

Under the title "materialization" are given such examples as the Lord God walking in the Garden of Eden in the cool of the day to commune with Adam and Eve, the appearance of the Lord to Abraham in the plains of Mamre, Jacob's wrestling with an angel, and other times when God manifested Himself to man. None of their references refers to a dead person.

Jesus expressly declared that God is a Spirit. Even so, Christians recognize that God has manifested Himself to humans at various times down through the ages, and in various manners. The appearances of Jesus to His followers after His death and resurrection is an accepted tenet of the Christian faith, but in no way substantiates a belief in the manifestation of departed human spirits. Paul specifically teaches that "to be absent from the body is to be present with the Lord." (2 Corinthians 5:8)

The Bible does list an incident at the transfiguration of Jesus when He walked and talked with Moses and Elijah, but when the disciples who saw this wanted to build three tabernacles, one for Jesus and one each for Moses and Elijah, the latter two disappeared and they saw no one except Jesus. A voice from heaven said that this was God's beloved son. "Hear Him!" Clear instruction thus was given that dead saints are not to be worshiped or "heard."

The Old Testament tells us that though witches had been outlawed by Saul, he disguised himself and sought help from the witch of Endor when he was unable to contact God. This is related in the twenty-eighth chapter of 1 Samuel.

Many Bible scholars claim that the medium did not contact Samuel himself but rather a familiar spirit, however the Bible says that it *was* Samuel. Note that even the witch was surprised—and frightened—when Samuel appeared. It seems logical that God stepped in and allowed Samuel to appear as a final warning to Saul, but not through the offices of the medium.

Under the title "spirit-writing," one reference given in the spiritualist tract refers to the handwriting on the wall seen by Belshazzar. Here also the sovereign God used supernatural means to warn man, but again, this is no basis for believing a departed human spirit did the writing.

Another reference to spirit-writing is when God inscribed the Ten Commandments. What folly to connect this tremendous communication from God with spirit-writing by dead people!

Under "trumpet-speaking," the reference is to the sound of trumpets heard when God was making His momentous visitation to Mount Sinai for the purpose of giving the commandments. Another is to the sound of a trumpet John the Revelator heard when he was being given the apocalypse, as stated in Revelation 1:10. In these instances the spiritualists are once more confusing God's sovereign power with communications from the departed dead.

Under "levitation" are cited Obadiah's fear that Elijah

162

will be caught away before he can report to the king; Ezekiel's being lifted heavenward for a tremendous vision of God, and Philip's being caught away by the Spirit from one place to another.

In this latter instance it is plain that Philip's spirit did not leave his body, but that God supernaturally transported both in order to perform His purposes. The Bible teaching is that "to be absent from the body is to be present with the Lord," and nowhere is there evidence that the spirit is free to leave the body and go walking around by itself, as spiritualists teach.

The section under "independent voices" includes the Lord speaking to Moses (Deuteronomy 9:12-13); to Samuel, (1 Samuel 3:3); to Ezekiel, (Ezekiel 1:28); to the disciples, (Matthew 17:5); to Jesus, (John 12:28-30); to Paul, (Acts 9:4, 7), and to Peter, (Acts 11:7-9). *All these instances refer to God communicating with men, not to contacts with persons who have died.*

This is also true of the section on spirit communications in dreams, which lists Jacob's dream of a ladder to heaven, Joseph's dream of being honored by his brethren, and Pharaoh's dream of seven years of plenty and seven years of famine. These are all records of God's dealing with men, not with communications from departed humans.

The Bible does not teach that there is no communication from the spirit world, but it does teach that this is not from humans who have died. It speaks of familiar spirits, and of evil spirits, and of the fact that Satan can perform supernatural acts. Evil spirits can pose as departed loved ones to delude men and women into following this devilish doctrine.

Any doctrine of life or any supernatural manifestation should always be weighed by the Word of God, and if it is not properly credentialed there, it should be discarded in favor of scriptural truth.

This way is clearly delineated in Isaiah 8:19 when the prophet asks, "And when they say unto you, 'Consult the mediums and the wizards who whisper and mutter,' should not a people consult their God?"

17

Secrets of a Satanist Priest

"If you're *really* a witch and *really* have power— let's see you burn that building down!"

This was the challenge presented to his older step- brother by a young San Bernardino, California, boy. It did not go unheeded!

"I put a spell on the building, which was a bar," says twenty-five-year-old Mike Warnke. "That night the grease in the kitchen overheated and the place caught fire. It burned to the ground."

What he had said in jest had come to pass. The young boy was convinced: Mike's power was real.

From this incident Mike, too, became convinced of his powers as a witch. As verification Mike related story after story regarding happenings in which he later par- ticipated. In fact, his influence brought him to the post of Master Counselor in one of the largest Satan worshiping organizations in Southern California.

For reasons of his own, Mike has asked us not to use the name of that organization, which is reputedly still in existence.

I came into contact with Mike when he was a cardio- pulmonary technician in the United States Navy. He has since been discharged from the service. The story Mike has to tell is bizarre.

An orphan boy with a "catch-as-catch-can" religious background, while still a teenager he became the revered high priest of a 1500 member Satanist cult.

His story is not a pretty one, even omitting episodes so secret they are still known only to him. Because of his former involvements there is always the possibility that something violent might happen to Warnke.

Mike told us that his father was a six-times-married, small-time hood and dope pusher who died when Mike was eleven years old. His mother had already been dead for three years, and his stepmother at that time was a nineteen-year-old girl who beat Mike with a dog leash.

Memories of his early childhood in Tennessee are not happy. There was lots of drinking, and he remembers his father driving around with a machine gun on the car seat beside him. Once his father's car was machine gunned while Mike was in it.

He remembers being threatened by adults that he would turn out "just like your dad" if he were not careful.

After his dad's death, Mike went to live with two aunts for the remainder of the school year. When he was twelve years old he went to live with a half sister, who was much older than himself, and her husband. They became "Mom" and "Dad" to him and he still holds them dear, though at times their relationship has been rocky.

Mike helped launch troubles within this new family as soon as he arrived at their California home. They were Catholics. The conflict was largely due to the difference between Mike's past religious background. His staunch Church of Christ aunts had armed him with anti-Catholic literature and ample warnings as to Catholic heresy.

As soon as Mike arrived he informed his new family they would all die and go to hell because they were Catholics, and that furthermore the pope was the Antichrist.

His new family did not insist he become a Catholic, but they did insist he learn what Catholicism was all about. So they enrolled him in St. Francis de Salles Catholic School in Riverside.

Starved for a mother's love, Mike there came under

the kindly influence of Sister Mary Frances, a Dominican nun whom he describes as the sweetest woman he has ever known. Other sisters and one of the priests also impressed him quite favorably, and he quickly became interested in the mysticism of the church.

The language of the Mass, the rituals themselves, the vestments and miter all captured the admiration of the youngster, and he became completely involved in the church. He links his need of a mother image with his adoration of the Virgin and says he began to spend hours upon his knees before the statues.

The youth made all *A*'s in religious subjects and began planning to enter seminary. In fact he did attend classes there during the summer.

Religion, however, began to interfere with his social life, and he slowly drifted away. His foster parents drank frequently, and he started drinking and dating frequently.

Then he entered San Bernardino Valley College and changed his appearance: his hair grew long and he bleached it white, he purchased weird clothing from rummage shops, and began to frequent coffee houses. Soon his heavy drinking became a real problem, and he turned into a teenage alcoholic. After a while alcohol no longer "did anything for me," as he recalls—and he was ripe for the scene which followed.

A friend offered him some marijuana. Though he at first refused, he began using it with his roommate to avoid being an outsider. This was in 1965 and preceded what he refers to as his "short but brilliant" career in dope and witchcraft.

Mike began to get loaded with drugs frequently, and even ate "pot" on his food. Next came his experiences with peyote, mescaline, "reds," and "speed."

Dr. Timothy Leary's defense of the use of LSD fascinated him, but he also felt to use the psychedelic drug was scary. He approached it rather cautiously at first as member of an authorized college control—group experiment. However, he liked his first experience so much he began to trip regularly. Then he was introduced to the needle at a party, and found he had gone from smoking pot to shooting heroin in little more than two months.

Formerly a husky, good-natured guy, he began to neglect food and dropped to a weight of around 110 pounds. His school work also suffered, and he became a drop-out from his classes. He continued to hang around the campus to hold discussions under the trees with other pseudo-intellectuals, and to pursue his new career of pushing dope.

The same friend who turned him on to marijuana and who had been supplying his dope needs now went a little further and invited him to a party. About eighteen or twenty people were involved. The proceedings began with the use of dope and degenerated into a sex orgy. This orgy took place in San Bernardino, in a palatial home on a hill overlooking the city.

"It was one big sex deal, indecent, perverted," he recalls.

About this same time Mike began transporting dope and carrying messages for those involved in dope-running and in other secret practices. One day he found himself initiated into a Satanic witchcraft organization.

A barn in an orange grove was the site of the coven's rituals, which were similar in structure to the Catholic High Mass. A stone altar, which had grooves cut in it to catch the flow of blood, stood before an inverted cross. A goat head idol was in evidence, and a pentagram, where spirits came after they were summoned during various incantations. Part of the service included participants offering themselves to the devil.

The coven could call up three messengers or spirits at each of these rituals and send them to execute any task. Some covens had as many as six messengers working for them and could call them up by name, Mike says.

When a hex was proposed, one of the members would mention what they wanted done, and others would vote on it either by raising their ring hand in assent or placing the hand flat on a table to dissent. The coven ring, worn on the index finger of the hand, has a design featuring a left hand with a crescent and star in the palm.

If the verdict was to afflict a certain person, the group would invoke the spirits with incantations and would "get a presence."

"You could feel it," the youth said.

"Some people could be hexed without all this rigamarole simply by the power of suggestion and their own superstition," Mike said, "but some couldn't be buffaloed, and we had to use powerful stuff."

The "powerful stuff" can be demonstrated by what happened to a college professor who had irked the group. The coven sent demons to oppress his children. These children began experiencing mysterious pinches which left them with bruises. The father could even see the pinching being done as the skin raised and turned purple, but the pinchers were unseen. In addition, cultists branded a star into the wooden front door of the professor's home. The professor contacted the worshipers, and after he promised a cease-fire, the spirits were called off.

Mike quickly became deeply involved in the practices of witchcraft, to the extent that his brother claims he saw Mike in trances at various times when his body would become so stiff that he could be supported by neck and heels as his body was placed between two chairs.

Possessed with the proverbial "gift of gab," Mike advanced rapidly through the ranks of the coven until he became one of the three master counselors in the group.

Because he was the ritual high priest, he presided at all meetings. He also arranged parties to lure other people into the organization through dope and orgies, and succeeded in promoting membership growth from 500 to 1,500 members.

His organization friends included two college professors, a high city official, a high police official, and a practicing physician who often acted as their doctor.

His Satanist group was more or less overseen by an elite ultra-secretive and highly financed group known as the Illuminati, rumored to be a widespread ring of Satan worshipers involved in an international conspiracy to pave the way for the rise of the Antichrist.

There were three degrees of membership in Mike's organization.

The first involved private parties with "little satanic overtones" where minor rituals were used as a prelude to orgies.

Next were secondary rituals used on minor occasions for "the binding together" of members in fellowship. "Sort

169

of a Sunday-go-to-meeting sort of thing," Mike explains. These were held in a warehouse.

The third level of participation in the coven involved the satanic rituals of the group, including blood sacrifices and ritualistic murders. These required the use of a nude female as a simulated sacrifice. After going through the motions of disembowelment, the members would cut the head off a chicken instead and let the blood run over the woman's body.

Mike says he saw convicted killer Charles Manson at such a ritual once and that Manson "thought he was being shortchanged. He favored actually sacrificing the person." He described Manson as being a person who "bugged everybody he was around. He was too intense. He made people nervous." And, he added, "Manson had bad eyeballs."

Mike described another ritual which included the use of "red bread" and "red drink." The "bread" was flesh, and the "drink" was blood.

The flesh eaten was usually that of a human finger which had been whacked off with a hatchet. No one was forced into offering a finger, but several were willing to do it as a sacrifice to the devil. Mike says it was an honor among Satanists to have one or more fingers missing. After the ritual, the person was taken to a physician friendly to the coven. This doctor also was used for other medical purposes, such as when members of the coven would deliberately break someone's hands.

Often representatives of the mysterious Illuminati would show up, always well-heeled and driving flashy cars, according to Mike. They usually came to observe, but they made the priest nervous.

"When they weren't around, I was the big cheese and had the power," he says, "but when they were there everybody catered to them. I felt like a fish."

Acceptance into the Illuminati was considered the "goal" by these Satanists. Once in that organization, you "really had it made." Mike claims he once saw an Illuminati pay out $150,000 in cash in a dope deal.

It was believed the Illuminati were behind many mysterious events. For example, when a satanic priestess in Gardena went beserk and hurt some people, it was believed that Illuminati money served to hush the deal and bail the girl out.

Prompted by the Illuminati, Mike's coven arranged an automobile "accident" for a man who had quit the organization. After his release from the hospital, this man quickly rejoined the club.

It was also believed that the Illuminati were behind a three-day conference held in Manhattan which Mike attended. This particular conference stressed refining the rituals, and one complete day was spent in acting out and refining the rites. This conference was held in the huge home of a man believed to be an Illuminati agent.

Other conferences Mike attended were in Salem, Massachusetts, and in San Francisco, California.

In Salem, the witch in charge was Bridget Bishop, who claimed to be a descendant of one of the Salem witches. Her claim is that the people burned at the stake were not the witches; the real witches were the ones who stirred up the trouble.

The San Francisco conference was called by the Church of Satan in January of 1966 and had newspaper coverage, although most Satanist activities were ultra-secretive in those days.

It was here, among other places, that Warnke saw Manson. Though he did not see Anton LaVey at this event, he had seen him at others and described him at that time as "panhandling around the edges."

During this time, Mike was living it up to the hilt. He had two apartments with rent completely paid, furnished as extravagantly as he wanted. A seemingly endless supply of funds was available to him for whatever he desired. He was supplied with a car and driver, and a "servant" whose main function seemed to be to acquire money for him if he needed anything. He was also given $3,000 worth of new clothes, lot of books, and "plenty of broads and booze." He particularly enjoyed being driven around in the silver Continental at his disposal. This high living was made possible, according to Warnke, because the group controlled the illicit dope market in the area.

"Satan supplied my needs," Mike adds. "Many people who believe in God don't believe in the devil, but I would pray to the devil, and he would answer. I was in Satanism for what I could get out of it. Everyone in it was there for some reason of gain. All of us were greedy for something."

One member he especially remembers was a highly intellectual, beautiful, and wealthy girl, who was power hungry. Others were in "for kicks." Even students who hung around avowedly to study the group became trapped in its vicious society and lost their objectivity. Warnke knows of only two who were able to maintain their objectivity and get out in time.

"It wasn't really so much *the worship* of the devil as it was a *partnership* with the devil," Warnke maintains. "You give him what he wants, and he gives you what you want. The only thing is *you always have to pay him back*, not only when you die, but right here."

The wages Warnke had to pay were high, but he claims it was poetic justice. He lost everything he had even faster than he had acquired it. How it happened was simple.

He became sick. One day he was so sick that he couldn't even prepare his own "fix." A girl friend did it for him and in so doing, overdosed him. He almost died. In as impersonal a way as possible, Mike's former associates came to his rescue.

Stripped naked, he was dumped out of a car at the emergency entrance of a private hospital. Since Mike was obviously without funds the hospital would not treat him. Instead he was transported to the county hospital and admitted there under the name John Doe after he refused to tell his real name. It took eight days for him to "dry out," but before that he knew the gang was through with him.

Among the "friends" who had dumped him off at the hospital was the man he had succeeded as master counselor and Warnke's "servant," who became his successor.

When Mike was finally released he discovered that all his clothes and furnishings were stolen, and that the money and friends of the past were both gone. He managed to scrounge up just enough funds to buy an unregistered Smith and Wesson .38 police gun with one bullet.

He was in the midst of composing a suicide note when

he heard some Christians pass by, singing happily. Their joy made him so mad he decided not to commit suicide.

Instead he went to the nearby Navy recruiter and signed up to be inducted into the service immediately. Since the recruiter was trying to fill a quota he helped get Mike's police record waived so he could be inducted.

After getting off the bus at boot camp, however, Mike had a change of heart and tried to get back on the bus. The driver refused to take him back to town.

His enlistment was a delight to the sergeant, who ordered Mike's shoulder-length white hair to be shorn, leaving one long strand like a queue. Mike was ordered to Scotch tape this strand to his head at night so it would not be torn out by mistake. The hair became a source of constant embarrassment to him.

Also an irritation to him were two barracks mates, Tom and Bob, who enticed him into attending chapel with them. Afterward Mike ridiculed the chapel service, but he could not overlook the deep concern Tom and Bob continued to show him.

Still suffering drug withdrawal flashbacks, Mike was frequently violently ill. He would perspire so much his bedclothes would become soaked, leaving him wet with chills. Then Tom and Bob would hang his blanket up to dry and give him theirs, despite their own discomfort. They would also get up and bring him a glass of water when he needed it.

One night when he was on fire watch, Mike toured the barracks and noticed how restless the other men were in their sleep, moaning and tossing about. Only two, Tom and Bob, slept like babies.

Mike noticed one of them had left a Bible open where he had been writing a letter home. The pages were open to John 3:16, a portion of Scripture dear to the hearts of Christians: "For God so loved the world, that He gave his only begotten Son, that whoever believes in Him should not perish, but have eternal life."

Mike figured he had tried everything else and decided there and then to become a Christian. Only nineteen years of age, yet with hideous experiences already on his conscience, he hid in a mop closet, put his head down on his arms on top of a mop bucket and prayed to God.

Mike did not go to bed the rest of that night. Instead he sat on his bunk praying to God and reading the Bible. The next morning he was grinning, with a happy glow on his face. Tom and Bob knew then that something had happened to him. The three young sailors began to have prayer and Bible studies together as the two older Christians gently led Mike into spiritual growth.

His family also knew something had happened to him when he went home on leave. He got along with everyone!

One day on a hometown street, Mike and a buddy encountered Sue, a girl he had known in school and who was a Christian. She had a friend, Laurie, along, and soon she and Mike began dating. Later, however, he married Sue, and continued his career in the Navy as a medic in Vietnam. During his tour of Vietnam duty he received eight distinguished service medals including the Vietnamese Cross of Gallantry and the Purple Heart.

"You might hear someone say that they are a white witch or a gray witch," he says, "but there's no such thing as a good witch. They make witchcraft their business, and they use bait to get people involved. They use everything from drugs right on down to 'harmless little parties.'

"Many people think it's a game. Maybe if I'd known what it was like, I wouldn't have become involved. My friends were injured, my wife was injured, my parents were endangered. It's only because of Jesus that I was able to get out."

Even since then he has been attacked both by spirits and by humans in an effort to get him to rejoin the organization.

"You can't just pay lip service to the devil," Warnke warns. "With him it's cash and carry. I gave him people, and he gave me what I wanted—money and a good time."

However, when the money and the good times were gone it was the Lord Jesus who gave him forgiveness of sins, peace in his heart, and his Christian wife and son.

18

Meditation—Trip to Chaos

The stranger who stood at the door of Roger Houtsma's apartment in Sacramento, California, was somber.

"I have come to teach you advanced techniques of meditation," he told the younger man.

Roger was eager to learn new techniques. In the days before consulting gurus and practicing yoga became the fashionable thing to do, he had been led to the meditation scene through experimentation with LSD, tarot cards, and astrology. Now he was ready for something deeper.

As the stranger seated himself lotus-fashion on the floor, the expression on his face was transformed from one countenance to another with breathtaking rapidity before Roger's startled eyes. Finally the alterations ceased, fixing on one face in which the eyes were "an effervescent light," Roger said.

"That white light entered my body through my eyes and filled the inside of my being," Houtsma recounted later. "It was very spacious. From that moment on I knew that this spirit had taken over a portion of my will. After that, things would happen and I would do things—over which I had no control."

This was just one of a number of weird manifestations

Roger experienced in a search for reality which almost lost him in the dark jungles of the occult and severely threatened his sanity. His frightening mystical experiences culminated in actual demon possession.

Roger is an extremely intelligent young man, and this alone made him fair game for intellectual pursuits, and a quest into the intangibles of this world. In addition, he says that his own personal hang-ups contributed to the journey.

"I guess what first led me in the direction I went was the realization of my own personality problems," Houtsma said. "I was bored with the middle-class American ideal in which I was being raised. I didn't find any personal desire for the goals which were offered me, nor did I have any real meaning or purpose in life. I was interested in things that were more of a challenge.

"I found myself having a great deal of conflict with my parents. I became very rebellious, and I found I didn't want to play the game anymore. I wanted to choose my own games.

"I was not a satisfied person; I was not happy. I didn't have inner peace, and my only objective, starting around the ninth grade, was to find inner peace."

Early in his search, he came into contact with what was known as the beatnik movement. He read books which led him into a new life style that seemed compatible with what he was seeking.

The trail led him to the study of Zen Buddhism and other Eastern religions, and he began to study psychology.

"I looked right down into the basic beginnings of all psychology," he reports. "It doesn't take long for anyone who studies psychology at all to run the implications out to what they are being taught. People are finding today more and more that there is a tremendous similarity between psychology and the things taught in the basic Eastern religions, Buddhism and Hinduism.

"If you run psychology out to its ultimate end, it leads you towards the development of a changing level of consciousness, and an altering of consciousness. For example, you begin with hypnosis, dreams, and things of that nature. If you have a good subject for hypnosis, you can put him

176

into transcendental states very easily, bringing him back into his early childhood."

After entering college, Roger began to realize that most of the professors did not know any more than he did as far as an ultimate answer for existence was concerned. So he began to explore on his own.

"At this time in my life blues and jazz were very important in my life," he says. "This goes along with the whole school of 'beat' thought at that time. I was enjoying the spirit of darkness that was in the music. It really expressed what was in my own heart—the feeling of frustration and alienation, yet the desire for change through a freedom of expression."

At that point he began using marijuana "to enter altered states of consciousness," and the use of pot led him into experiences spoken of in many Eastern doctrines. His interest in Buddhism, Hinduism, and in Tibet and Tibetan literature increased. He dropped out of school and went into a deep study of these subjects while still using drugs.

"In early 1965, I began taking strong psychedelics; they opened my understanding of the spirit world. I can honestly say that intellectually I had never acknowledged the existence of a spirit world until I experienced LSD. Then I knew that there was a spiritual world, and that when people spoke of God they were speaking of this dimension of life. I began to search further in this direction."

After his LSD experiences, Houtsma believed that the true spiritual revelations were hidden from the masses, and revealed only to an inner circle of communicants who were able to achieve the proper "awareness."

He began meditating, even taking the "short path" which he described as very dangerous. "You can freak out into what even Hindus feel to be possession by evil spirits," he said.

He now believes this is what happened to him, at the depth of his involvement, when one day a man came to his door and wanted to teach him new techniques of meditation.

After that experience, Roger made pilgrimages to Mount Shasta in California where followers of the esoterica believe there is a concentration of power and energy. From here, they claim, it is possible to be transported in the spirit to the Himalayas.

Roger says his meditation trips included spirit-walking and floating-sensations—even without the use of drugs. He believed, and still does, that it is possible to relax the body so much that there is no need to breathe or to have a heartbeat. He also believes it is possible for the soul to leave the body in what is known in occult circles as astral projection. He says that he himself reached the place where his heart would beat only once about every five minutes.

Roger describes these experiences as frightening, because he did not have complete faith in what he was doing. Doubts begin to enter his mind as to whether or not he would return to reality after his astral experiences.

He began to doubt his spiritual leaders and also began to wonder if these spirits and experiences were of God. If not of God, what *was* the source of these strange experiences?

Roger had met the widely publicized spiritual master Maharishi, but he describes the occasion as being "a big disappointment." The Maharishi, he complains, violated the basic principles of all esoteric teachings and "commercialized" his beliefs. Roger felt that religion should not go to the masses, but that the truly hungry person should come to the religion.

The Bible was used by mystic leaders, but was twisted to present the particular view they desired, Houtsma said.

He asked one teacher what he thought of Jesus.

"Jesus Christ was right," the teacher said. "He said, 'I am the way' and he was right. I (*pointing to himself*) am the way."

Roger liked the fact that the Self-realization Fellowship incorporated Jesus Christ in their meditation program, but he felt this group also had commercialized their message, and this didn't set right with him.

All during this time, Roger really felt he was in communion with God, despite the fact that he made his living selling dope as well as using it himself.

One LSD trip left him in such a state that at his wife's

suggestion he went to see a minister who prayed for him. Roger feels that at this prayer session he had an "experience" with Jesus Christ, but not a real "revelation" of Him.

Up to this point, Roger's religious background was sketchy. He had been to a Presbyterian Sunday school several times when he first started elementary school. Later as a school boy he was enticed to a Baptist church under the ruse that he would see a magic show.

He remembers the show, a visual aid presentation on how Jesus can change the heart, but he also remembers how he felt "duped into going there." He saw much inconsistency in the lives of Christians, claiming most of them had hang-ups and were worse off than he was because at least he admitted his, while they did not.

The experience he had in the minister's study didn't "take," however, as Roger says he "lit a joint" on the way home and decided he did not need to change his ways.

He had noticed that most religions, except for outright Satan worship, acknowledged Jesus in some aspect. The Eastern cults felt Jesus was "tuned in" with God, but only Christianity taught that Jesus actually *is* God.

Roger began to hunger for an encounter with Christ. He sought through meditation to meet with both Yogananda, founder of the Self-realization Fellowship, and with Jesus.

He says he "cried in the spirit" for such an encounter, and one day it happened. During a meditation trip, he says he saw Yogananda clearly, and then Jesus faded in from the background. Jesus was walking away from Roger in apparent rejection of him.

"I was pained and shocked," Roger said. "I knew intuitively that Jesus was rejecting me."

Immediately he snapped out of meditation. The suddenness of the reaction is ordinarily an experience he describes as dangerous, painful, and capable of causing serious physical damage. Roger was unharmed despite the potential consequences.

The next three months preceding the real revelation of Jesus to him is described as "prenatal" by Roger, a period of growth and development. Within him grew a great desire to see Jesus face to face. Everything else in life lost its purpose and meaning.

Finally Roger turned away from his yoga master in complete rejection. This time he asked Jesus to be his master. Roger still had reservations, though; he could not accept Jesus as the Son of God. Later, when he *did* realize who Jesus was in this relationship, it meant "a whole new life, a renunciation" for Roger.

"I took the step. I had a revelation of Jesus Christ. I've known no separation from Him since." This is the ringing testimony Roger gives today.

"There is a real need for young people to have a revelation of Jesus Christ *by the Holy Spirit*," he says. "Experiences can be duplicated, and might even be out-matched, in the occult spirit world. One might have an experience but get no real deliverance at all."

All was not a bed of roses following his conversion, however, as his mind had been severely damaged through his meditation trips. After hours of prayer and of seeking God with his wife, eventually Roger explains that his mind was healed. He was able to think clearly again.

Afterwards on several occasions, the spirits which had controlled him sought to attack him. In one instance, he and a friend were praying in a church when the spirits began to "whoosh" around. Roger describes the feeling as if an air hose was shooting forceful streams of air over his entire body. Ministers who had been in the living quarters behind the church came out, began to pray with him, and the spirits left.

At another time in his apartment he went into deep meditation against his will. "I couldn't stop it," he said. "I couldn't talk." God revealed to a friend his need for help, and the friend came in and began praying for him.

This time, Roger said, there were "five levels of deliverance," each one accompanied by a guttural scream from his own mouth. After the fifth and last scream, he felt released.

Finally, Roger was able to obtain what he calls real and lasting victory over these recalcitrant spirits. In communion with God, he was told his guru would never return to him again, and an angel was being placed to guard him from further attacks.

Of his deliverance Roger says, "I didn't feel anything. So often we think the deliverance of God is going to be a big sensation. I didn't feel anything at all, but the work was done. Never again have those spirits returned to me."

Roger found in Jesus Christ alone what he failed to find in Christianity-at-large in his earlier years and in his meditation trips. Now twenty-five years old, he is striving through his testimony to make an impact upon those who might be drawn into the same error and dangers of drugs and meditation trips.

At present he is a minister in Sacramento where God is mightily using him.

An integral part of reaching and holding seeking youth, Roger believes, is for the church to get a firm grasp on the "mystical realities" of serving God, the things which "have been played away from during the past generation in most churches." These, he says, include "the inward path to the working of the cross, the fellowship of Christ's sufferings, conforming to His death, the mystical union of the body of Christ, and the mystery of godliness—all of which have been neglected in the organized Christian churches."

He adds, "The one who has been on drugs knows of mystical experiences. He's already aware of spiritual realms which are largely ignored by the church."

Fundamental Christian authorities agree that yoga and meditation trips are totally opposed to what the Bible teaches, and therefore should be completely avoided by the Christian. In addition to these teachings which Roger says should be emphasized by the church, an important one which should not be overlooked is the baptism of the Holy Spirit.

Attempts have been made to divide systems of yoga into various stages. The first of the stages deals with gymnastics, breathing and relaxation exercises, and meditation. The second involves control of the subconscious, the third has to do with controlling the forces of nature, and the fourth is concerned with the mastery of magic and the cosmic forces.

Experts have testified to the seeing of amazing phenomena in the various stages, including practitioners stick-
ing knives through their flesh without drawing blood,
melting ice by concentration, and the starting of fires.

The first stage of yoga sometimes has been described
as harmless and has been recommended by physicians in
treatment of certain patients.

Dr. Kurt Koch, an authority on the subject who has
counseled 20,000 occult cases with success, says that
"yoga may indeed be harmless to begin with, but it
ends dangerously. Even the first stage of Yoga is not
without its dangers, when, for example, the exercises involved are linked with short Buddhist prayers."

He revealed that students taking part in exercises are
often required to repeat short Indian phrases which upon
inquiry turn out to be such sayings as "Buddha is the
enlightened one" or "Buddha is supreme."

Dr. Koch said that practitioners involved in Yoga for
years who have come to him for help have admitted that
the final phase of Yoga is a matter of pure demonical
practices. He strongly counsels Christians to avoid any involvement in the system.

"What need," he asks, "have we as Christians of the
inner 'edification' of these pagan Eastern systems? Have
the Scriptures no more to offer than Buddhism or Hinduism?"

"We insult our Lord when we leave the living source
of the Bible for these foreign springs whose poisonous
contents either kill or paralyze our spiritual lives."

Many people who delve into the metaphysical realm
say they are searching for truth.

If they are sincere, *really* searching, and really want
the *truth*, their search will lead them to Christ.

Pilate asked Jesus, "What is truth?" but he didn't
stop to settle the issue.

People who ask that question, "What is truth?" may
mean a variety of things.

One may ask that question and not really *care* what
the truth is. They use that as an excuse to continue in darkness.

Another may ask "What is truth?" and indicate that

the truth is unknowable, an intangible with no answer.

But the soul who asks "What is truth?" and means it with the whole heart, will find the Christ who said, "*I am the truth*." (John 14:6)

John 8:32 says, "And you shall know the truth, and the truth shall make you free."

The person who really wants to know the right way can find assurance in John 7:17, "If any man will do His will, he shall know of the teaching, whether it is of God," and also in 1 John 1:5 which says, "In Him there is no darkness at all!"

Christ is the truth, the way, the life, the answer!

Man need look no further.

19

Origin and Activity of Demons

We have seen in these chapters how Satan can strike at all ages through the occult. He deceives both the rich and the poor, the educated and the ignorant, the sensuous person and the intellectual.

We have seen how, through the occult, men and women come under the influence of satanic spirits to such an extent that they do unspeakable vile and violent things, many of the victims even becoming demon possessed.

What are demons, anyway? Where do they come from? What is their purpose?

I've seen people do mischievous things sometimes and then jokingly remark, "The devil made me do it."

That's not amusing to me. It is too true. And yet people don't realize that they are being influenced, controlled, and directed by demons. It is possible to be oppressed and vexed by demons as well as being possessed by them.

Demons can actually take possession of human beings and animals. They can talk or cry with a loud voice, using the lips and tongue of a person; they can torment people, they can stand, walk, and seek rest. They can and do tell lies. They make people believe lies.

Demons tell fortunes. They can cast a person to the

ground and cause him to foam at the mouth. They can deceive people into making wrong decisions or depress people into suicide. They can cause physical affliction in a body or mental anguish in a mind.

Satan was once the "anointed cherub" in the Holy Mountain of God. Ezekiel 28:13-15 gives a vivid description of Satan's position with God before his fall:

You were in Eden, the garden of God;
Every precious stone was your covering:
The ruby, the topaz, and the diamond;
The beryl, the onyx, and the jasper;
The lapis lazuli, the turquoise, and the emerald;
And the gold, the workmanship of your settings and sockets,
Was in you.
On the Day that you were created
They were prepared.
You were the anointed cherub who covers;
And I placed you there.
You were on the holy mountain of God;
You walked in the midst of the stones of fire.
You were blameless in your ways
From the day you were created,
Until unrighteousness was found in you.

The iniquity found in him was pride—which caused him to want to exalt his throne above the stars (Isaiah 14:13-14):

But you said in your heart,
"I will ascend to heaven;
I will raise my throne above the stars of God,
And I will sit on the mount of assembly
In the recesses of the north.
I will ascend above the heights of the clouds;
I will make myself like the Most High."

Satan wanted to be equal to the Most High! Isaiah 14:12 says, "How you have fallen from heaven, O star of the morning, son of the dawn!" The repercussions to Lucifer, now known as Satan, are described in Ezekiel 28:16-19:

By the abundance of your trade
You were internally filled with violence,
And you sinned;
Therefore I have cast you as profane
From the mountain of God.
And I have destroyed you, O covering cherub,

From the midst of the stones of fire.
Your heart was lifted up because of your beauty;
You corrupted your wisdom by reason of your splendor.
I cast you to the ground;
I put you before kings,
That they may see you.
By the multitude of your iniquities,
In the unrighteousness of your trade,
You profaned your sanctuaries.
Therefore I have brought fire from the midst of you;
It has consumed you,
And I have turned you to ashes on the earth
In the eyes of all who see you.
All who know you among the peoples
Are appalled at you;
You have become terrified,
And you will be no more.

Jesus says in Luke 10:18, "I was watching Satan fall from heaven like lightning."

Tuck that scripture in your mind, for I am going to get back to that verse shortly to make a very telling point against the devil!

Anyway, Satan fell, and many wicked angels or spirits followed him.

He is now cast out of heaven, his former glory gone. God has permitted him some power for a little while. However, Satan knows his days are numbered, and he knows what his end is.

Revelation 20:10 says, "The devil who deceived them was thrown into the lake of fire and brimstone . . . and will be tormented day and night forever and ever."

Satan knows the Scriptures. Many times he even uses them, but he always twists them, or takes them out of context, or stops short of their real point. He hates God!

Satan has always wanted to strike back at God, but his problem was how to do it. How could he "get even" when God is invincible? There was no way to overpower God, nor to hurt Him personally.

Then one day God made man.

On all the other days when God created something—the light, the sun and the moon and stars, the trees and vegetation, the fish and fowl—the Bible tells us that God saw that it was good. Read that in the first chapter of Genesis, the very first chapter in the Bible.

But when God made *man*, then it says that "God saw all that He had made, and behold, it was *very* good." (Genesis 1:31)

You see, God made man as the "apple of His eye," (Psalms 17:8). Isaiah 49:16 says, "Behold, I have inscribed you on the palms of My hands."

God created man for His glory. Isaiah 43:7 tells us so. "Every one who is called by my name, And whom I have created for my glory, Whom I have formed, even whom I have made."

God loved to commune with man. We are told in Genesis that He came down in the cool of the day to talk to Adam in the Garden of Eden.

See the diabolical scheme being born in Satan's mind? There *was* a way to get back at God! He would strike at His creature! He would get back at God through man, who was *not* invincible, but vulnerable! He would defile that one who was supposed to be God's glory, and he would destroy that communion between God and man!

Satan struck through jealousy, through his spirit of rebellion and deception, enticing man to disobey his Creator. He didn't just strike once. He has devoted his whole career, thousands of years, to destroying all that is good in man —his body, his mind, and his spirit—and disrupting the communion man might have with God. He has done it both by outright attack and by his most cunning wiles! But he *has* done it!

Realizing that his end is at hand, Satan is leading his final, all-out attack on man in these last days. He's trying everything possible to undermine God's best creation.

Reverend J. Finis Dake, noted contemporary Bible scholar, has advanced the interesting thought that heaven is the capital of the universe since it is where God's throne is, and that earth is a planet in rebellion against God. The rebellion is being led, of course, by Satan!

The truth is that Satan does have legions of wicked

angels or spirits which he commands, and they *are* in rebellion against God, and they *do* attack people.

Jesus spoke of Satan as having a kingdom in Matthew 12:26 which says, "And if Satan casts out Satan, he is divided against himself; how then shall his kingdom stand?" The devil is the ruler of the multitude of wicked spirits named in Ephesians 6:12. These are rulers, powers, world-forces of this darkness, and spiritual forces of wickedness in heavenly places. He is called the "prince of the power of the air" in Ephesians 2:2, the "ruler of the world" in John 12:31, and the "god of this world" in 2 Corinthians 4:4.

So you see, he does have power.

He also has intellect. He knows Jesus, and he knows the plan of salvation.

One thing he doesn't have is good morals. That's why his demons are sometimes termed "unclean spirits," and his influence leads to immoral conduct. That is why demons seek to inhabit human bodies, so that they might work out their indescribable lusts and evil longings.

If demons are cast out of someone, they will seek to reenter the same body, inviting other demons to join them.

> Now when the unclean spirit goes out of a man, it passes through waterless places, seeking rest, and does not find it.
>
> Then it says, "I will return to my house from which I came;" and when it comes, it finds it unoccupied, swept, and put in order.
>
> Then it goes, and takes along with it seven other spirits more wicked than itself, and they go in and live there; and the last state of that man becomes worse than the first. That is the way it will also be with this evil generation. (Matthew 12:43-45)

In the fifth chapter of Mark and the eighth chapter of Luke, we are told how Jesus cast demons out of the madman of the country of the Gerasenes. When He asked the spirit his name, the reply was "My name is Legion; for we are many."

The spirits requested that Jesus allow them to go into a herd of swine instead of being sent out of the country. When this request was granted by Jesus, the unclean spirits went out of the man and entered into the swine. The entire herd, composed of about 2000 swine, then ran down a steep place into the sea of Galilee and were drowned.

Demon spirits can cause physical disease and demon possession. Sometimes mental derangement is due to demon possession, but not always. A tract put out by the Gospel Tract Society gives a list of symptoms which may indicate the presence of demon activity, although some of these symptoms may stem from other causes.

The manifestations they list include prolonged depression or gloominess, indifference, irresponsibility, unpredictable behavior, delusions, uncontrollable passions, sexual perversions, enslavement to drugs, alcohol, or tobacco, compulsive eating, as well as uncontrollable temper, hate, or other psychopathic tendencies.

Demonic presence frequently can be traced to people who have chronic fear anxieties, nervousness or neurotic behavior, feelings of inadequacy or self-pity, abnormal desires for attention, extremely negative personalities, compulsions (lying, stealing, gambling), obsessions (fear of dying, acute jealousy), and thoughts of self-destruction.

Further symptoms of activity are psychic experiences, possession of psychic or extrasensory powers (none of which are to be confused with genuine gifts of the Holy Spirit), and psychic oppression (seeing apparitions, hearing voices, poltergeist phenomena, etc.).

A good indication of demonic activity is indifference to spiritual things such as Bible reading or prayer, chronic doubts or difficulty in exercising faith, unscriptural religious beliefs or practices, hatred of the blood atonement, and blasphemous thoughts against God.

Others include abnormal talkativeness or loudness, muttering to oneself, shunning others, unkempt appearance, abnormally bright or glazed eyes, perverse or defiant facial expression, chronic physical ailments that do not respond to prayer or treatment, serious marital or parental problems, and strife or discord in the church.

Jesus treated cases of demonic possession as realities. He is not only described as "charging," "rebuking," "commanding," and "casting out" the unclean spirits, but He addressed them directly and on several occasions held conversations with them!

When Jesus was beginning His public ministry in

Capernaum, Mark tells us in the first chapter, verses 23-26:

> And just then there was in their synagogue a man with an unclean spirit; and he cried out,
>
> saying, "What do we have to do with You, Jesus of Nazareth? Have You come to destroy us? I know who You are—the Holy One of God!"
>
> And Jesus rebuked him, saying, "Be quiet, and come out of him!"
>
> And throwing him into convulsions, the unclean spirit cried out with a loud voice, and came out of him.

The New Testament furnishes in the fullest details the manner in which those tormented or possessed by demons may be set free. In ordaining his disciples, Jesus clearly gave them the ability to cast out demons.

Luke 10:17 reports that the seventy disciples Jesus sent out to go before his face into every place he planned to go returned again with joy, saying, "Lord, even the demons are subject unto us in Your name."

In the sixteenth chapter of Mark, we are told in verse seventeen, "And these signs will accompany those who have believed: in My name they will cast out demons."

The biblical cure for demon possession was always the same. It did not consist of magical means nor formulas of exorcism. The key was *the word of power* which Jesus spoke, and which He entrusted to His disciples, which the demons always obeyed. Matthew 10:1 says, "And having summoned His twelve disciples, He gave them authority over unclean spirits, to cast them out, and to heal every kind of disease and every kind of sickness."

The depths of occultism from which God can deliver those who trust in Him can be attested to by Shirley, a young lady who came to our Action Center in San Diego (a rehabilitation center I started some time ago in San Diego to help young people). For ten years Shirley had been so deeply involved in the spirit world that she began to think she was God.

Shirley had always had an interest in the occult but her actual involvement began when she was thirteen. Prior to that, she had received little religious training but had attended a Catholic boarding school for one year.

Her interest in the occult started with magic card tricks and sleight of hand. She began devouring books on astrology and immensely enjoyed horror stories. For her birthday someone gave her a set of tarot cards which caught her interest.

She read a great deal, and graduated to "heavier stuff," the trail leading her into the Brotherhood of Light, an Egyptian cult which she contends is "about as heavy as you can get." She also got into Zen Buddhism and astral projection, an occult experience where the spirit leaves the body.

"I was really possessed with demons," she says, and adds that the occult experiences gave her a feeling of god-like power. While practicing occultism, she also used drugs and "had unearthly visions, including dragons in the sky."

She became interested in a philosophy which taught that God and Satan were the same power using different vibrations, and that there had to be evil in the world to balance the good.

"I actually thought I was God manifested in a female body," she said, "and I even thought I was going to change sex." She said she knew others who had experienced these same manifestations, and many who felt they were Jesus Christ.

"I became so demon possessed that I could project power across a room to attract attention or to move objects," the young women said.

Despite all this, she still described herself as a "white witch" who was not out to hurt anyone.

Finally, she flipped out on drugs on such a "trip" that it took her three months to come off it.

At this time she was living like a gypsy, sleeping in the woods, and telling fortunes with cards. Her mode of travel was hitchhiking, and she hitched rides "traveling as a guy." She carried her Brotherhood of Light bible and was prepared to win people into that belief.

One day a Christian lady picked her up, witnessed to her about the Lord and asked her to accept Jesus.

She accepted the Lord at the Christian's invitation and "meant well." However, a few days later she took some drugs and became so violently ill that she was hospitalized. As she recovered, she found a Bible in the hospital room and began to read it. The Word of God struck home.

"I knew this was the truth, and I began preaching it to people right there in the hospital," she said. "After that I had no interest in horoscopes or card reading. I knew then that these things were of the devil, and I put them all aside."

Since that time, the devil has tried to attack her in various ways, but filled with the Holy Spirit and reinforcing her stand with Christian fellowship, prayer, and daily Bible reading, she is standing for God and helping others who have been similarly involved.

Her deliverance was similar to that of Larry Dennstedt, a twenty-six-year-old former occultist, from San Diego, with the exception that Larry's experience did not include drugs. Even when drugs were slipped to him without his knowing it, they never affected him, he said. This, he felt, was due to "stronger powers" within him.

He had become aware of these powers "somewhere between the ages of six and twenty-two."

"It was a growing thing," he said, "and began when I turned against God at the age of six." One year later, he made an actual decision to have nothing to do with God.

At an early age, Larry said, he realized he could read people's minds and started to become absorbed in the supernatural. He was made aware of reincarnation beliefs at the age of eighteen.

It was also at that age when he became conscious of a great thirst for God.

"I quit college and started my search," Larry said. "I wanted three things: a reason to live, a person to live for, and to find out if God were real. If I could find no answer to these things, then. . . ."

The next three years of searching took him to many different states and brought him into contact with all types of people and cultures. His path included white magic, black magic, spiritual intuition, fortune telling, reincarnation, Rosicrucian studies, person-programming, spirit-walking, levitation, palm-reading, numerology, karma omission, witchcraft, séances, Satan worship, hypnotic thought-transfer, card-reading, and astrology.

Finally he recognized that "there was a God or gods."

"I knew He had a plan for me and loved me and wanted me to follow Him," he said. But still he rejected Jesus and the fact of the virgin birth.

During this time, he was praying to God to use him. Yet at the same time, he was trying to help people with whatever supernatural power he had. Finally he realized he was not helping others but rather hurting them.

"I would lose control of myself and go into a trance," he said. "When I came out of it, I found out I had destroyed people."

He began two years of active persecution of Christian churches by breaking up youth services.

"All that time I knew they had something going for them," he said. "I used to love to make Christians cry, but I couldn't deny that after they prayed they came back stronger than before."

His prayers became more desperate. "Lord, will you use me?" he would cry out! Before he realized it, he had added the request, "Jesus, come into my life!" Immediately he knew something had happened, and instantly he lost all of his occult powers!

"No one laid hands on me, no one rebuked the devil, but Jesus instantly set me free, totally free!" he testified. Later he received the baptism of the Holy Spirit and gained new insight into what had happened to him.

He has had battles, of course, but four years after being delivered, Larry is still going strong for the Lord and has helped scores of other young people who have been involved in the occult. He has been invited to many public schools to give his testimony on the delivering power of Christ.

Any reader who may be involved in the occult to any degree can know the same delivering power, for God has said in His Word that whoever the Son sets free is free indeed. (John 8:36)

"The Son of God appeared for this purpose, that He might destroy the works of the devil." (1 John 3:8)

20

More Than Conquerors

Even while the final chapter of this book was being edited, there came to my office one of the most pitiful pleas for help which I have ever heard! George Ekeroth, executive director of World Evangelism, talked to this lady. Her original letter is on file now at my office. It is just one of hundreds we receive showing the tragic results of venturing into Satan's spiritual realm on his terms.

Here is her letter just as she wrote it.*

> In the name of God, help us!
>
> Can you help end spiritual torture on a good family, torture caused by a spiritual path?
>
> All my life I had a longing and finally knew that longing was for God when I saw an ad for "God Awareness, God realization, those who talk to God follow this path" [It was from the Eckankar system which Paul Twitchell supervised in America]. I answered the ad and worked hard for two years, unsuccessfully, trying to learn to soul travel, yearning to find God for my family and me.
>
> My husband, who was a child prodigy, with 168 I.Q., had ESP at the age of two and astrally projected at the age of five, and for our four wonderful children (now seventeen to twenty-six years of age).

---

* Editor's note: The confusing thought patterns have not been altered.

In October 1967, I went to the first world-wide seminar of Eckankar expecting to learn to soul travel. At a private spiritual consultation, where the student is naturally under the spiritual protection of the guru and the path, Paul Twitchell said, "What can I do for you?"

I said, "Teach me to soul travel." Instead of soul traveling, I was completely destroyed, was removed from my mortal body fifty minutes out of sixty, a pornographic posture came from him and he fell off his pedestal as a guru. A pornographic question was said *through* me. (I *know* I did *not* say it myself.) His immediate answer was "Why not?"

The next day the voices of Paul Twitchell and his guru were inside of me and the start of a nightmare of four and one-half years, tortures of my spiritual family and my spiritual selves, forty-two in my spiritual family and thirty-nine of us with mortal selves living and I am the only one who answered the Eckankar ad.

Their screams of agony inside me and outside, pictures of their tortures put in front of my spiritual eye, tortures on their astral bodies by Paul Twitchell and the evil one, and tortures in the Akashic records, and tortures on them from the Akashic records, physical torture on their astral bodies, tortures much worse than the atrocities of the Nazi concentration camps.

I got *no* help from Paul Twitchell or the path of Eckankar —his answer to my letters about the tortures—"An Eck Chela cannot be harmed."

My husband and our children have been removed from their bodies; and I have been removed from mine *many* times even for three full days once when I had taken off a week from secretarial work to try to find a way to end the terror. I have had three psychiatric clearances to use for a court case, so you know the trouble is not mental.

In July of 1970 it was *proven* to me that I was 100 percent manipulated by the spiritual world, some good and some evil. When the ones manipulating me left me, my eyes were open and remained open (no blinking whatsoever,) I could not close my eyes, could not even *try* to. I could not talk or move. My head was hanging on my chest until they again manipulated me.

Since then it has been proven to me a hundred times (about) that I cannot open or close my eyes, cannot think or talk or move, act, react or counteract in any way whatsoever. I can see only. All else is put through me by the spiritual world.

At one time, all feeling and life left my feet up to about four inches above my ankles (lifeless, like clay). I have no silver cord, but am not permitted to tell you how I am kept alive. At another time, it felt like Paul Twitchell "emptied" my head leaving only my skull. For the first time in my life I had no dreams at night.

It has been terror, agony and torture for my wonderful spiritual family, my spiritual selves, my mortal family and my mortal self, four and one-half years of voices inside and out at almost every waking moment; when my boss is dictating at my secretarial work at times, when I am reading the Bible looking for the "universal truth behind every religion and path" at times, talking through me aloud on the subway, along the street, in front of my children, etc., often evily. I have been to many, hoping for a healing, but there has been none. Can you help or do you know where I may be able to get help for all of us?

From the spiritual world to me, about me and therefore maybe about all, there has been duplicity, insidiousness and almost *no* truth because the evil one talks through everyone in the third dimensional spiritual world in and around me, and therefore may be all over as well and there is no truth in Akashic records, completely fabricated by the evil one. Paul Twitchell says we can change our own Akashic records in the future so you know they can be fabricated past, present, or future.

In the name of God, help a desperate spiritual family and a drowning mortal family!

I know this letter sounds like a fairy tale. But it is a reality—and the sad part is that this letter is representative of thousands who have given themselves over to the occult scene or outright worship of Satan.

This lady is desperate, but thank God, there is help for her and all who will *fully* and *completely* turn to the Lord Jesus Christ.

This is a spiritual battle. Satan isn't fooling. He's not playing patty cake. He may act like he's playing just to get you "hooked," but it is a trap.

An early chapter of this book told you that *you* are Satan's target. Well, you are also *God's target*. If you do not know the victory and safety which can be yours in

Christ, I trust that this book will inspire your faith to reach out and take hold of the precious promises of God. All of them are geared for victory. God has made *no* provision in His Word for the defeat of His creation.

Christ is over all and above all. All power is given unto Him in heaven and in earth! More astonishing is that He has passed this power on, that through Him we are *more than conquerors* over all the works of the enemy! Romans 8:37 says, "But in all these things we overwelmingly conquer through Him who loved us." This promise is not for when He comes again, not for when we get to heaven. But this promise is for *now*—for *here*—in this present world!

There are some simple but dynamic steps you can take towards full and continuing victory:

1. GET RIGHT WITH GOD.

If you are troubled about this matter of witchcraft and occultism in any respect, the first step to victory is to make sure that *your heart is right with God.*

We are no match for the devil in our own strength. We might recognize him, fear him, hate him . . . and still be under subjection to him if we fail to put on the strength of the Lord Jesus Christ. There are literally thousands of souls in this world *longing* to be free! If you, the reader, are one of them, *now is your hour!*

There is no other way to be reconciled to God except through the atoning work of the Lord Jesus Christ on the cross of Calvary. Salvation is through faith in the finished work of Christ who came into the world to seek and to save that which was lost!

He is the only Mediator between God and man. You cannot rely upon the spirits of the dead or other supernatural manifestations. You cannot be led by the stars or the turn of a card or the line of a palm.

When by faith we behold the Son of God as our Savior, the Spirit of God does a work of *regeneration* in our hearts that makes us new people, new creatures, people at peace with God. We are "born again" into the family of God, and He has become our Father in reality. The third chapter of the book of John describes this "born again" experience to us. John 3:16 says, "For God so loved the world, that He gave His only begotten Son, that whoever believes in Him should not perish, but have eternal life." If you don't know Jesus as your Savior, stop right here. Ask Him to come into your heart, to forgive your sins, and to be your Lord.

2. KNOW THE WORD OF GOD.

God has given us certain tools whereby we may live an overcoming life. The Bible is one of the main tools. It is the Word of God. His promises are "yea and amen" to those who believe. Get it established in your heart that this Word is infallible and unchanging. It is just as real and powerful today as it was when holy men of old put it in writing under the inspiration of the Holy Spirit!

The Scriptures were the tool that Jesus used in his effective defeat of the devil when the enemy tempted Him. This amazing story is found in the fourth chapter of Matthew when Jesus Himself was tempted of the devil in three different areas.

Each time, Jesus' response began with, *"It is written!"* and then He quoted the Scriptures, completely defeating the enemy with God's Word!

We are told in this fourth chapter of Matthew that Jesus was led of the Spirit into the wilderness where He fasted forty days and forty nights.

When He was hungry, the devil came to Him and said, "If You are the Son of God, command that these stones become bread."

Verse 4 tells us that Jesus answered and said, "It is written, 'Man shall not live on bread alone, but on every word that proceeds out of the mouth of God.' "

Satan next took Him to the pinnacle of the temple in Jerusalem and told Him, "If you are the Son of God throw yourself down; for it is written, 'He will give His angels charge concerning You; And on their hands they will bear You up, Lest You strike Your foot against a stone.' "

Jesus' answer this time was, "On the other hand, it is written, 'You shall not tempt the Lord your God.' "

The devil then took Jesus to a high mountain, from which he showed Jesus all the kingdoms of the world and the glory of them, saying, "All these things will I give You, if You fall down and worship me."

Jesus used the resource of God's Word again when He said, "Begone, Satan! For it is written, 'You shall worship the Lord your God, and serve Him only.' "

Then the devil left Jesus and angels came and ministered to Him.

The same resource Jesus used is available to us. We can know and believe and stand on the Word of God—and Satan will *have to flee*!

I cannot stress strongly enough the need for Christians to be grounded in the Word of God.

The Bible tells us in 2 Timothy 2:15: "Be diligent to present yourself approved to God as a workman who does not need to be ashamed, handling accurately the word of truth."

Remember that Satan, too, can quote Scripture, and his workers often do likewise, twisting the words to their own ends, taking them out of context, or using partial truths.

This was the case in one of the temptations of Jesus mentioned above, when Satan took Christ to the pinnacle of the temple and urged Him to jump. Satan quoted from the ninety-first Psalm when he said, "It is written, 'He will give His angels charge concerning You; And on their hands they will bear You up, Lest You strike Your foot against a stone.' "

Satan's quote, however, stopped short of the next line of that Psalm, which pictures triumph over the enemy: "You will tread upon the lion and cobra, The young lion and the serpent You will trample down." This is just what Christ will do to Satan in the end!

It is important to know the Word of God, the *whole* Word, and to understand it correctly. The Holy Spirit Himself helps us with this!

3. GUARD YOUR THOUGHT LIFE.

This is very important. Even though we need to

know about Satan and his power and to be aware of the dangers of the occult, undue preoccupation with this knowledge can become an actual avenue for Satan to work. Constant dwelling on the power of Satan does not create a healthy soil for the growth of Christian virtues and may lead to soul-destroying imaginations.

I have known people who became so entranced with the operation of evil spirits that they began to see evil spirits in everyone!

The Scripture tells us to think on the power and purity of God and on things which are good.

Philippians 4:8 says, "Finally, brethren, whatever is true, whatever is honorable, whatever is right, whatever is pure, whatever is lovely, whatever is of good repute, if there is any excellence and if anything worthy of praise, let your mind dwell on these things."

4. SHUN ALL ACTIVITES RELATED TO SPIRIT WORLD ENCOUNTER, HOWEVER SEEMNGLY HARMLESS.

The road to spiritualistic involvement in occultism is easily traveled, as pointed out in this book. It can start with a game, such as playing with an Ouija board "for fun," or with fortune-telling cards in the family parlor.

"Innocuous" witch-oriented television programs may give moments of worldly enjoyment, but they tend to make viewers tolerant, even sympathetic, to so-called "white witch" practices.

Witchcraft is not funny, even when practiced by "white witches" or accomplished by an innocent-looking young housewife who can cast a spell or conjure up a long dead relative by wiggling her nose.

The horrendousness of occultism is pinpointed time and again in the Bible, which does not differentiate between white and black witches. Serious students of witchcraft doubt that such a difference exists. Even when witches seemingly use their powers for good, experience has shown the end result is evil in its scope.

Enjoyment of witchcraft and Satanism movies can reach the point where the horror is not turned off as easily as the television set. Nightmares and delusions have been known to follow the viewing of such films, and murders have been committed by unstable people who later explained, "I saw it in a movie."

The forecast in the daily astrological column of your newspaper is potentially harmful. Millions of intelligent people will not make a move without consulting their daily horoscope.

I have pointed out how forecasters frequently disagree among themselves and contradict one another. In another instance the managing editor of a Los Angeles community newspaper chain at one time picked his astrological column for a given day at random because the release dates of the columns did not coincide with his publication dates. Readers who took the column seriously were plotting their activities on the "wrong" days on an editor's whim!

How much better it is to seek guidance for the day's activities in prayer and devotional Bible reading each morning. This way the material is always timely and the Source unimpeachable. Psalm 37:23 reminds us that "the steps of a man are established by the Lord."

5. LIVE A CONSISTENT SPIRIT-FILLED AND PRAYERFUL LIFE.

An on-again, off-again attitude toward living for Christ will not suffice in these last days when the spirit of antichrist is rampant.

In Ephesians 6:12 we are told that "our struggle is not against flesh and blood, but against the rulers, against the powers, against the worldforces of this darkness, against the spiritual forces of wickedness in the heavenly places."

Therefore we must "take up the full armor of God, that you may be able to resist in the evil day, and having done everything, to stand firm." (Ephesians 6:13)

6. TAKE YOUR STAND AND KEEP IT BY THE POWER OF THE HOLY SPIRIT!

Jesus defeated Satan once and for all at Calvary. By His atonement there He provides victory over *all* the power of the devil.

A few pages back I told you to tuck a Bible verse into

your head and that we would refer back to it. That verse was when Jesus said, "I was watching Satan fall from heaven like lightning." (Luke 10:18)

I want you to look at the circumstances regarding what was happening when He said that. Read verse 17 again.

The seventy that Jesus had sent out returned again "with joy, saying, 'Lord, even the demons are subject to us in Your name.' "

That's when Jesus pointed out how the devil had been cast out of heaven. He is an *already defeated* enemy! Look at the following verse, where Jesus told these disciples, "Behold I have given you authority to tread upon serpents and scorpions, and *over all the power of the enemy!*"

Furthermore, before Jesus ascended to heaven to be with the Father, He promised the outpouring of the Holy Spirit. He told His disciples to tarry until they were endued with power from on high. (Luke 24:49) In Acts 1:8, He promised, "But you shall receive power when the Holy Spirit has come upon you."

In Acts 2:39, speaking of the gift of the Holy Ghost, Peter declares that "the promise is for you and your children, and for all who are far off, as many as the Lord our God shall call to Himself."

That means us! That means me! That means you!

The battle is spiritual, but *we* have the greater Spirit. We don't have to face Satan's tanks with water pistols. We have the spiritual atomic bomb!

First John 4:4 tells us, "Ye are from God, little children, and have overcome them; because *greater is he who is in you*, than he who is in the world!"

If you have experienced this great victory that is ours in Christ Jesus, this thrilling in-filling of the precious Holy Spirit, we can close this book together "giving thanks to the Father who has . . . delivered us from the domain of darkness, and transferred us to the kingdom of His beloved Son." (Colossians 1:12-13)

I have just finished a small booklet entitled "How to Win the Battle of Life." I would like to send this to you free and postpaid as a gift to help you gain the rich spiritual experience necessary to face the onslaughts of Satanic powers in our day.

I know this booklet will lead you step by step through the many vicissitudes and pressures that face us in the complex world in which we live. Thank God there is a solution for every problem, for every need in our life . . . and we can win the battle of life.

Write me:

> Morris Cerullo
> P.O. Box 700
> San Diego, Calif. 92138

Epilogue

The Battle of Life*

"Then the Philistines seized him and gouged out his eyes; and they brought him down to Gaza and bound him with bronze chains, and he was a grinder in the prison house." (Judges 16:21)

The American family today is facing a tremendous crisis. One out of every three homes ends up in the divorce courts. In my state of California, the actual percentage is higher. It is creeping very close to one marriage out of two ending up broken and divorced.

It's no longer a sin for our families to see headlines about people who have been married two, three, four and five times.

Crime in 1966 rose some 14 percent in America, and in 1967, 16 percent. According to figures released from the FBI in Washington, D.C., by 1968 crime increased nearly 28 percent in America. Each year it gets higher.

I don't think that anybody needs to be convinced that it's not safe to walk in a park at night or even in the dark streets of your home town.

A man told me about some friends of his who were

---

* Editor's note: This is a sermon preached by Reverend Morris Cerullo.

205

at a convention in Washington, D.C. They had been out walking the streets at 11 o'clock at night to get a breath of fresh air.

The next day they were talking with a convention hall guard, and told him about their walk.

"Man! You're crazy!" The officer got excited. "Don't you know that it's *not safe* to be out at 11 P.M.?"

The visitors didn't believe him.

"Do you mean in the capital of the United States that the streets aren't safe after dark?"

Now, these are not statistics that we like to talk about—but they are real statistics.

We are caught up in a battle, a tremendous battle of life.

Now, let's look at this world.

There are two forces in this world. One is the force of good. The other is the force of evil.

The good force is God's force.

The evil force in our society and in our world, whether you want to accept this truth or not, is a satanic force. It is the power of the devil.

His power is real; and only the power of the devil could grip our society to turn young men and women into dope addicts.

That's why there is only one deliverance, and that deliverance is the supernatural power of the Holy Spirit of the living God.

Now this world in which we live is governed by laws.

There are really only two basic laws that govern the world. One is the natural law. The other is the spiritual law.

One is the natural law of humanity, science, and nature.

The other is the spiritual law of God.

Now there is a parallel truth about both of these laws. It is that you must not violate them.

If you do violate these laws, you will pay the supreme price for doing so.

Let me illustrate.

For example let's say that I do not choose to believe in the law of gravity—although it is a natural law governing the universe.

Let's say that I defy that law. I get on top of the music hall auditorium and people gather in the streets and say, "There's Morris Cerullo! Isn't he the man who says the law of gravity does not exist or that it is not real?" Meanwhile I jump off the music hall roof.

Do you know what is going to happen to me? Of course you do. They will pick up the bloody remains of Morris Cerullo from the sidewalk.

There is something strange about this natural law, and that is this: You do not have to *believe* in it. It simply exists. Gravity is there whether you believe in it or not. You can say, "I don't believe in the law of gravity," but it's still there. Saying that it does not exist does not remove its operation.

Then there is the law of self-preservation. A man must eat to live. If you did not eat for two weeks, three weeks, four weeks, or even five weeks—then your body would begin to disintegrate.

This is the law. It is a natural law, and it is a proven scientific law; it is a basic law of nature. It's like this: You don't have to *believe* that you have to eat to stay alive; all you do is eat. But break this law to nourish the body, defy it, and see what happens. You will die.

There is a law of self-preservation that I obey when I'm in the great crusade meetings which God has given me. I perspire heavily when I preach under God's anointing, and I get out of my wet clothes as fast as I can. I don't stand around and talk to people in my wet shirt.

Why? Because I cannot defy the law of nature in my body. That law says that if I get a chill, tomorrow I will have laryngitis. Tomorrow I will suffer from a cold, no matter how much I believe in divine healing.

I cannot break the natural laws. If I break them, I will pay the price, I will pay the penalties.

Now there are also spiritual laws of God, and their truth runs parallel to the natural laws. You do not have to *believe* in the spiritual laws anymore than in the natural ones.

You do not have to accept the fact that there is a God.

You do not have to believe in the Ten Commandments.

You don't have to be a Jew. You don't have to be a Baptist. You don't have to be a Methodist. You don't have to be a Pentecostal.

You can be an absolute atheist if you want to, but that *will not remove* the spiritual laws of God.

The exist, and if you break His laws you will pay the supreme penalty for doing so.

The spiritual law is described in a three-letter word. It is the *sin* law of God.

"The wages of sin is death." (Romans 6:23)

"The soul who sins will die." (Ezekiel 18:4)

"Whatever a man sows, this he will also reap." (Galatians 6:7)

These are the spiritual laws of God.

"You shall not steal, you shall not bear false witness, you shall not commit adultery, you shall not murder, you shall not take the name of the Lord. . . ." These are some of the spiritual laws of God. They're in the universe as much as the natural laws. Break the laws and you'll pay the price.

That is what the battle of life is all about.

The battle of life is between these two forces: the force of good, God's force, the force of evil, which is the devil's force.

I want you to look at your life.

There is not a man, there is not a woman, there is not a boy, there is not a little child who is not caught up in this battle of life.

A psychiatrist tells us that in every person there is a dual personality.

Have you ever wondered why a little child can act one way to a person at one time and then turn around and act in a completely different way at another time?

Mothers sometimes throw their hands up in the air and exclaim, "I thought I understood my child, but I don't!"

You see, in all of us there is a dual personality, and one personality wars against the other. We have a personality of good and a personality of evil; the personality of the image of God, and the personality of the power of the devil.

208

It boils down to the fact that in every person *there is the potential of becoming the person that God Almighty wants you to be.*

God has a purpose for your life. There lies within you the possibility and the potentiality of rising up and becoming the person that God wants you to be.

Now there is another possibility, and that's where the battle of life comes in.

There also lies within us the possibility of becoming what the devil would like us to be.

You see, the possibility of being what God wants us to be is there and the possibility of being what the devil wants us to be is also there.

The battle of life is between the force of good, God, the force of evil, the devil. One is trying to get us to be one thing and the other is trying to destroy the purposes that God intended for our lives.

There was a man in the Bible by the name of Samson who went through this battle of life.

God had a purpose for Samson's life.

Samson was born according to a prophecy that he was going to come. From his mother's womb Samson was set aside as a Nazarite. The vow was carried out, because of this, that a razor *would not* touch a hair of his head all through his life.

What was the purpose of God for Samson's life?

One, he was to be a judge in Israel. Two, Samson was to be a spiritual leader, a spiritual giant.

Samson was to sit upon the throne and the people of Israel were to come to him with their problems, with their needs, with their distresses. He was to be the man who would be anointed by God to deal with the problems, to give guidance, to give wisdom, to rule, and to judge. That was his destined position.

But Samson was caught up in this battle of life.

He was caught up between what God wanted him to be, a servant of God, a man who would hold his head up high and walk down the street anointed with the power of the Spirit of God.

But the devil also had a purpose for his life.

That's the purpose the devil has for you and that's

209

the purpose the devil has for me. He wants to take us and make us a nothing; an absolute nothing.

This is what the whole Bible's life is all about. God says, "You shall not . . . you shall not commit adultery. You shall not bear false witness. You shall not take the name of the Lord your God in vain. You shall not . . . ! You shall not . . . !" The law of God!

This is what the battle of life is all about: it is between the law of God and the law of that spirit of man's sinful, rebellious nature that rises up and says, "I shall!"

Somebody says, "Brother Cerullo, we're not under law."

No, we're not under law. But did you know that under the law in order for you to be called a murderer, you actually had to have a witness see you kill the person— to see you take the knife and put it in his back?

You had to actually be caught in the act of murder.

Even today, if you are convicted of first degree murder, you can't be sentenced by circumstantial evidence to the gas chamber or the electric chair.

Not so with God's law. That was under the Old Testament.

Do you know what God says under the New Testament? God says, "Every one who hates his brother is a murderer." (1 John 3:15)

All you have to do is to have envy in your heart.

All you have to do is to sit in your church and think evil thoughts of Mrs. Q. or John Jones or Suzy Boo Hoo or the preacher, and you've already committed murder in the sight of God.

You see, under God's law of grace we are judged by different standards than under the Mosaic law.

Did you know that before you could be called an adulterer under the law you had to be caught in the act of adultery? Did you know that? But not so in the law of God.

Even with our divorce courts today they have to set it up so that somebody will break in on the man and the woman before they can get a divorce on the grounds of adultery. Somebody has to break in that room and catch them in that act or catch them together. But not so with

God's law. Do you know what God's law says? God says, "Whoever looks upon a woman to lust [or vice versa, whenever a woman looks upon a man to lust], has committed adultery already in his heart!" (Matthew 5:28)

Samson was caught up in this battle of life.

Between what? Between the force of God and between the force of the devil. Between being what God wanted him to be and being what the devil was trying to make him be.

God said, "Samson, don't you go down and take those strange women." God said, "Don't do it," but Samson with his appetite and Samson with his rebellious, sinful nature turned his back on what God wanted him to be and said, "I will."

And the battle of life was on.

Sex happened to be Samson's weakness. I don't know what yours is. But I'm here to tell you this, as God's servant, that the devil will attack your weak points. He'll not come after you where you are the strongest, but the devil will come after you where you are the weakest.

Remember what I tell you. The devil has only one purpose in life and that is to make you look so sick before God that your life will amount to absolutely nothing. That's the whole purpose of the devil.

The story of Samson illustrates something else I want to make clear. You don't turn your back on good all at once; young men do not become dope fiends all at once. They start to play with sin. After they play with it and play with it to get bigger and bigger kicks, suddenly addiction gets hold of them and they can't cut loose.

This is what happens in the battle of life.

Samson met a woman by the name of Delilah, and he went down and he began to live with her and commit adultery with her.

The Philistines came to Delilah and said, "We understand that you've got Samson right under your thumb."

She said, "I sure do. He is so bound to me and what I can give him, and what we can do together, that he's forgotten that he ever was a servant of God. He's *my* servant now." What a testimony!

You know the story of how she tried to find out the

211

secret of his spiritual life. You read it in Judges, the sixteenth chapter.

First he lied to her. He said, "Bind me with green cords."

Then he lied to her again and said, "Bind me with new rope."

And then he lied to her again and said, "If you take the locks of my hair and weave them all together, I will be as weak as any other man." Three times he lied to Delilah.

You play with sin and do you know what will happen? As a born-again Christian, many of you have dabbled with sin. First it entered into your mind and you began to look on it. You began to think on it, and you began to meditate on it until it absorbed more of your thinking and more of your faculties, and you began to yield to it more and more, and more and more.

The Bible says that to whatever spirit you yield your members, to that spirit you become a servant to obey. You play with sin and you break the spirit law of God and you know what will happen? You will even give away your spiritual experience.

Some of you people are sitting here in this auditorium tonight as backsliders. You know what I'm talking about. You have played with sin. You have dabbled with it, and slowly you have slipped away from God until you have completely turned away from Him and sold out the blood experience, and the cross, and salvation for a little mess of pottage.

Samson did it. Delilah came to him finally and she said, "Samson, you lied to me all these times, now get out of my house and don't ever come back again."

That was the straw that broke the camel's back.

He said, "I can't leave you, Delilah, I can't!"

Look at him. Can you see him?

God had a purpose for his life. He was to be a strong man. Here was a man who when he prayed miracles happened. Miracles took place under his ministry of prayer.

Can you see him now? "I can't leave you, Delilah. I can't go. Please don't send me away."

Can you see what sin does to the human life?

"What do you want me to do, Delilah?"

"Samson, tell me wherein lies your strength?"

"If I tell you, you won't send me away?"

"No, I won't send you away."

"All right, Delilah. I've been a Nazarite ever since I was born. It was prophesied before I came into this world that I would be born. A razor has never touched a hair of my head. If you were to cut off all my hair, I would be as weak as any other man."

It's the devil's business to make you think God does not mean what he says. As you are fighting this battle of life the devil will come to you and try to convince you to believe every kind of lie that there is. That's how he brought sin into the world through Eve and through Adam.

God said, " 'You shall not eat from any tree of the garden . . . lest you die.' " but the devil came along and said, 'You surely shall not die!' " (Genesis 3)

Belshazzar thought that God did not mean what he said until a hand slipped out of the sleeve and began to write on the wall, "—you have been weighed on the scales and found deficient."(Daniel 5)

Ananias and Sapphira didn't think that God meant what God said, and they lied to the Holy Spirit. They were carried out dead. (Acts 5)

God means what He says. "Whatsoever a man sows this he will also reap." "For as he thinks within himself, so he is." (Proverbs 23:7)

This is the spirit law of God. This is what the battle of life is all about. It's the devil's purpose to make you think God does not mean what He says and that you can get away with it!

Sometimes on the surface it doesn't look like the man has come to collect what is due, but it will happen. It will be visited on the next generation. It will be visited on your children. It will be visited on your children's children!

I pastored a church some eighteen years ago in New Hampshire. A young lady came to me. She said, "Pastor, will you marry me?"

I said, "Bring your young man to my office and I'll counsel with you."

She brought the young man in. I talked with him. He was an unsaved boy.

Young ladies, listen to me, because this is what the

213

battle of life is all about. I'm not talking to you out of a hard heart. I have a teenage girl eighteen years of age. I know exactly what I'm telling you.

I explained to the boy that this girl was a Christian and born again and Spirit-filled and that he was not saved, and the Bible says, "Do not be bound together with unbelievers." (2 Corinthians 6:14)

I told him that if he would give his heart to Jesus, I would pray with him. He got indignant and looked at me, and said, "Preacher, I was born my religion, and I'll die my religion." He named a certain faith.

I didn't argue with him. I turned to the girl in his presence and I said, "Don't marry him."

You see, I didn't have to pray before making my decision. The law of God is clear on that subject. Just obey the laws of God in life and you won't get in trouble.

They decided to get married anyway without my blessing. They went to get their license and blood tests.

He had been in the Navy, and the blood test showed that he had contracted a disease, during this time. Until he was cured, they could not be married.

This was another voice of God speaking. Nothing in life happens to you by chance. God is trying to help you win the battle of life with everything that He has. He's put it to our disposal that you might win the battle of life.

I'm not here merely as a man to preach to you because I want to hurt you. If you are going to be set free you are going to have to know the truth. My Bible says, "You shall know the truth and the truth shall make you free." (John 8:32) I'm here as a prophet of the Living God to declare unto you, "Thus says the Lord!"

This couple played with sin because they couldn't get married. They committed adultery, and she became pregnant. Off to West Virginia they went to get married, and when they came back some time later, she had her child.

I hadn't seen them all during this time, but then I got a telephone call. The young girl was on the other end of the line. She was sobbing.

When I arrived in this town we only had a handful of people, and the church was very small. In eight months' time, the church had marvelously grown, all through signs, wonders, miracles, the eyes of the blind being opened, and the cripples walking.

This young lady called me up on the phone and said, "Brother Cerullo, I've got to have your help."

I said, "What can I do for you?"

She said, "I can't tell it to you over the phone. Come to my apartment."

Mrs. Cerullo and I went on over to the apartment. I walked into the door, and there was a lovely little bassinet.

The young mother looked at me and said, "Brother Cerullo, I've seen you lay your hands on the blind in our church. The blind eyes open. I've seen you lay your hands on the deaf and the deaf ears open."

Then she pulled back the thin veil-like material from the bassinet to reveal her little baby boy.

She said, "Will you please lay your hands on my little child and pray for him?"

All over that little child were growths, little growths of flesh hanging by the dozens over the child's body and face.

The doctor had said that those things were so alive that if they operated to take them off, they would just grow back out. They only gave the little child so much time left to live.

I went to put my hands on that little child.

You may not understand this, but God said to me, "Son, take your hands off. How can you bless that which has been cursed?"

"Whatever a man sows, this he will also reap."

It's the devil's business to make us believe that God does not mean what he says.

Samson went to sleep on Delilah's lap and you know what happened. She shaved the hair off his head and called for the Philistines behind the curtain to come out. Samson arose as he did the other times. He began to shake his fist up in the air to feel for the power of the spirit of God to take on this group of Philistines.

As be began to feel in the air he couldn't understand it. Something was gone. He grasped into the air but something was gone. That anointing didn't come any more.

Oh, it came the first time. It came the second time. It came the third time. You see, God never does leave anybody all at once.

He's merciful, He's kind. Some of you have lived in sin, and God's even covered it up for you. Nobody even knows about it. He's been merciful! He's been merciful! *He's been merciful!*

There will come a time when you will raise your hand to feel that forgiveness and to feel that spirit, but it won't be there anymore.

The Bible says that Samson "wist not that the Spirit of God had departed from him." The Philistines took him, and look what they did to him. Remember the text I read you? This is what the battle of life is all about.

Look at him now. Look at him! A judge, a miracle worker, a powerful man in prayer, look at him!

The Bible said the Philistines took him and they put out his eyes. That's the first thing they did.

Let me tell you, sin blinds. It promises you great light and glory. Sin promises you a good time. You walk down the road with sin and it looks good when it starts. Then all of a sudden, you are blind and you don't know where you are going, where you have been. You don't have any direction at all because sin blinds!

When you play with sin you'll sell out your wife. You'll even sell out your children that you brought into this world. Once sin gets hold of you, you'll do things that will disgrace the people that are the most dear to you and closest to your heart because sin is that ugly. Sin blinds.

They not only put out Samson's eyes, but the Bible says they bound him with fetters of brass. Sin not only *blinds,* but it also *binds.*

Young ladies, don't play with sin in that automobile. Don't go that extra step, because sin binds.

Ask the person on dope. Ask the drunkard. Ask the man or the woman who has given his mind over to evil thoughts of lust and sex and perversion. Ask them how much they would give you if they could get free from it. Sin *binds.*

They brought Samson down to Gaza and put him in the prison house blind and bound. They put him to push a stone wheel around.

216

I hope you never forget this picture, young lady, every time you come close to breaking the law of God.

Young man, every time you come close to doing something that might be just a little questionable, I hope this picture sticks in your mind. I pray you'll never forget it.

Look at him: blind, bound, and grinding in the prison house! Grinding day in, day out, week in, week out, month in, month out, pushing that wheel around and around and around.

He has plenty of time to think now. He's got plenty of time to say, "If only I hadn't disobeyed God!"

He knows now that that pleasure of sin for a season his brothers and sisters whom he has disgraced. He is thinking about his mama and daddy who can't walk in this world any more with their heads up high because everybody says there go the mother and the father of that sinner who sold out the children of Israel for a little mess of flesh.

He's thinking about the disgrace he's brought. Sin always works like this. When you sin you not only hurt yourself, you hurt those around you whom you love.

Husbands hurt wives. Wives hurt husbands. Mothers and fathers hurt children. Then everybody has to suffer for the sinful things people do. Sin blinds, binds, grinds!

Look at Samson. He's a nothing—an absolute nothing. He was to be a prophet, judge, ruler, God's man, miracle worker. Look at him—*nothing*!

What road are you heading down tonight? Are you on that road where the devil will make you a nothing? Or do you want to be what God wants your life to be?

He's got a purpose for you, a high purpose, a noble purpose. He wants you to be able to hold your head up high in this world, to be decent, to radiate the blood and the power of the cross.

There are two heavens and two hells. If you will turn and surrender your life to Jesus Christ . . . backslider, if you will repent of your sins . . . so-called Christian, if you will get right with God, I can promise you without any doubt—heaven on this earth and heaven in the life to come.

I can also promise you this—rebel against God . . . the Bible says God's Spirit will not always strive with you.

217

God will cover your works. He will even cover up your sin, let you go back into the church, and let you talk in tongues. He'll cover up a second time, maybe a third time, and then like Samson, he will leave you.

Don't you think for one moment that God is destined to always shower his love on you. Absolutely not! There are people walking the face of this earth who will never, never, *never* be saved because they have sinned away their day of grace.

Why? Because God is not mocked. "Whatever a man sows this he will also reap!"

I said there are two heavens. There are also two hells. Resist God and you will have hell on this earth. Ask the dope addicts if they don't have hell on this earth.

If you continue to resist God in His convicting power, you'll have hell in the life to come.

The Bible says, "Let a man examine himself." Examine yourself right now.

As God's servant, I tell you that you can rise up and be the person God wants you to be. I don't care how far you have gone. I don't care what you have done or what you have yielded to or what you have succumbed to. I promise you upon the authority of God's Word that if you will cast yourself upon God, He will hear your prayer and forgive your sins and will heal your soul. God will make you right with Him *right now*—and you can go forward being the person that God intends for you to be.

Bow your head right now, as God is speaking to your heart by His Spirit through the pages of this book.

Ask Him to forgive your sins and wash away your failures. Ask Him to let the new life in Christ Jesus flood into your heart right now. Ask Him to fill you with the Holy Spirit so full that nothing of the devil can crowd in.

Get yourself a Bible and read it from cover to cover. Read it daily.

Learn to pray! Get hold of God in prayer for miracles in your life and others.

Get into a good fundamental Bible-believing church where the pastor and people know that God's power is a reality. Write to me and I will personally pray for you and your needs. I will also send you free of charge some additional literature which will help you to have power over the devil.

My address is Morris Cerullo, P.O. Box 700, San Diego, California 92138.

God bless this book to your heart and use it to His glory. Amen!

Bibliography and Source Materials

Adams, Marjorie E. Cook, editor. *God in the Classroom*. Westchester, Illinois: Good News Publishers, 1970.

Anaheim Bulletin. Anaheim, California.

Bach, Marcus. *Strange Altars*. New York: Signet Mystic Books, 1968.

Bayly, Joseph. *What About Horoscopes?* Elgin, Illinois: David C. Cook Publishing Co., 1970.

Bjornstad, James. *Stars, Signs, and Salvation in the Age of Aquarius*. Minneapolis, Minnesota: Bethany Fellowship, Inc., 1971.

_____. *Twentieth Century Prophecy*. Minneapolis, Minnesota: Bethany Fellowship, 1969.

Bodin, Edward Longstreet. *Mystery History*. Lakemont, Georgia: CSA, 1964.

Buckland, Ray. *Ancient & Modern Witchcraft*. New York: HC Publishers, Inc., 1970.

Central California Register. Fresno, California.

Cerullo, Morris. *The New Anointing Is Here*. San Diego: World Evangelism, Inc., 1972.

Chicago Tribune. Chicago, Illinois.

Christopher, Milbourne. *ESP, Seers, and Psychics*. New York: Crowell, 1970.

Culling, Louis T. *The Complete Magic Curriculum of the Secret Order G.B.G.* Saint Paul, Minnesota: Llewellyn Publications, 1971.

Daily Pilot. Costa Mesa, California.

DeGrimston, Robert. *Exit*. Letchworth, Hertfordshire, England: The Garden City Press Limited, n.d.

Demon Experiences in Many Lands. Compiled by Moody editors. Chicago: Moody Press, 1960.

Dixon, Jeane. *My Life and Prophecies.* New York: Morrow, William, & Company, Inc., 1968.

———. *Reincarnation and Prayers to Live By.* New York: Morrow, William, & Company, Inc., 1969.

Dolphin, Lambert T. Jr. *Astrology, Occultism, and the Drug Culture.* Westchester, Illinois: Good News Publishers, 1970.

Editor and Publisher, April, 1971.

Ernest, Victor H. *I Talked With Spirits.* Wheaton, Illinois: Tyndale House Publishers, 1970.

Exel, Jerry. *Jesus and the Spirit of Astrology.* Berkeley, California: World Literature Crusade, 1971.

Farrar, Stewart. *What Witches Do.* New York: Coward, McCann & Geoghegan, 1971.

Ford, Arthur. *Nothing So Strange.* New York: Harper and Row, 1958.

Freeman, Hobart. *Angels of Light.* Plainfield, New Jersey: Logos, 1969.

Fresno Bee. Fresno, California.

Fresno Daily Collegian. Fresno, California.

Gilbert, Dan. *The Cult of Devil Worshipers in Washington, D.C. and Throughout the World.* Washington, D.C.: Dan Gilbert, 1950.

Glasser, William. *The Identity Society.* New York: Harper and Row, 1972.

———. *The Gods and Their People.* Chicago: The Process Church of the Final Judgment, 1970.

Great Falls Tribune. Great Falls, Montana.

Hagin, Kenneth E. *Demons and How to Deal with Them.* Tulsa, Oklahoma: Kenneth E. Hagin, n.d.

———. *The Gift of Prophecy.* Tulsa, Oklahoma: Kenneth E. Hagin, n.d.

Healy, E. F., and Meara, J. F. *Moral Guidance.* Chicago: Loyola, 1942.

Holzer, Hans. *The Truth About Witchcraft.* New York: Doubleday, 1969.

Insight. June 8, 1971.

Kerr, John Stevens. *The Mystery and Magic of the Occult.* Philadelphia: Fortress Press, 1971.

Koch, Kurt. *Between Christ and Satan.* Grand Rapids, Michigan: Kregel Publications, 1962.

———. *The Devil's Alphabet.* Grand Rapids, Michigan: Kregel Publications, 1969.

LaVey, Anton Szandor. *The Satanic Bible.* New York: Avon, 1969.

Leek, Sybil. *Diary of a Witch.* Englewood Cliffs, New Jersey: Prentice-Hall, 1968.

Levin, Ira. *Rosemary's Baby.* New York: Random, 1967.

Lindsay, Gordon. *The Mystery of Jeane Dixon.* Dallas, Texas: The Voice of Healing Publishing Co., 1966.

Life. Year End Report on Books, 1971.

Lubenow, Gerald, and Kellogg, Mary Alice. "Satanism: A Practice as Varied as Its Practitioners." *Post.* October 31, 1971.

Lyons, Arthur. *The Second Coming: Satanism in America.* New York: Dodd, Mead & Co., 1970.

Martello, Leo L. *Weird Ways of Witchcraft.* New York: HC Publishers, Inc., 1969.

McLean, Gordon R. *We're Holding Your Son.* Westchester, Illinois: Good News Publishers, 1970.

Miami Herald. Miami, Florida.

Montgomery, Ruth. *A Gift of Prophecy.* New York: William Morrow, 1965.

The Montrose Ledger. Montrose, California.

The Moon Sign Book. Saint Paul, Minnesota: Llewellyn Publications, 1970.

National Enquirer.

New York Daily News.

New York Times.

Newsweek.

"Occult Oppression and Bondage—How to be Set Free." Gospel Tract Society, Inc. P.O. Box 1118, Independence, Mo. 64051.

Ostrander, Sheila. *Psychic Discoveries Behind the Iron Curtain.* New York: Bantam Books, 1970.

Parade. May 13, 1966.

Penn-Lewis, Jessie. *War on the Saints.* (Abridged Edition). Fort Washington, Penna., n.d.

People Magazine.

Playboy Magazine.

Plowman, Edward E. *The Underground Church.* Elgin, Illinois: David C. Cook, 1971.

Post-Journal. Jamestown, N.Y.

Psychic Adventurer.

Rascoe, Judith. "Church of Satan." *MaCalls*, March, 1970.

Roberts, Susan. *Witches U.S.A.* New York: Dell Publishing Co., 1971.

The Sacramento Union. Sacramento, California.
San Bernadino Sun. San Bernadino, California.
San Diego Union. San Diego, California.
San Jose Mercury News. San Jose, California.
Santa Monica Evening Outlook. Santa Monica, California.
Spiritualist Hymnal. Boston: R.D. Row Music Co., 1960.
Stern, Jess. *Yoga, Youth, and Reincarnation.* New York: Bantam Books, 1968.
Sumrall, Lester. *Bitten by Devils.* South Bend, Indiana: Lester Sumrall Evangelistic Assn., Inc., 1964.
_____. *Five Steps Toward Demon Possession.* South Bend, Indiana: Lester Sumrall Evangelistic Assn., Inc., 1964.
Thallasa. (High school yearbook). San Clemente, Calif.: San Clemente High School, 1965.
Unger, Merrill. *The Haunting of Bishop Pike.* Wheaton, Illinois: Tyndale House Publishers, 1968.
Up-look. A Morris Cerullo World Evangelism publication.
Usher, Charles H. *Satan a Defeated Foe.* Fort Washington, Penna: Christian Literature Crusade, n.d.
Wall Street Journal.
"What's Behind the Rising Tide of Occultism?" *Today.* December 27, 1970.
"Witchcraft, Magic, Astrology, and All That." *The Lutheran Witness.* March, 1971.
Wolff, Charles E. *Freedom Is Not Free.* Long Beach, Calif.: C. E. Wolff, 1970.
World Vision Magazine.
Wright J. Stafford. *Mind, Man, and the Spirits.* Grand Rapids, Michigan: Zondervan Publishing House, 1971.

All source material bona fide and available for reference in official files at the offices of Morris Cerullo World Evangelism, P.O. Box 700, San Diego, California, 92138.

Other material such as cassette tapes and photocopied documents are not listed but also in the author's possession.